YOUTUBE SUCCESS IN 30 DAYS

A Beginner's Step-by-Step Blueprint to Build an Audience, Create Viral Content, and Make Money Online

---

BRIAN CHESSON

Contents

Week 4: Growth, Income, and Long-Term Strategy

Bonus Section: Resources to Help You Create With Confidence

Introduction

So, you're thinking about starting a YouTube channel, or maybe you've already uploaded a few videos and want to approach things more intentionally. Either way, you're exactly where you need to be.

In 2026, YouTube is more than a place to upload videos. It's a discovery engine, a creative platform, and a long-term opportunity for building an audience, sharing ideas, and creating real income. People from all backgrounds are using YouTube to grow personal brands, launch businesses, and turn skills or interests into something meaningful. And the good news? You don't need expensive equipment, a massive following, or to have everything figured out to begin.

You just need a clear starting point.

Throughout this book, you'll also find small reflection prompts and questions. These aren't tests: they're there to help you think more deeply about your goals, your process, and your progress. The more honestly you engage with them, the more you'll get out of this journey. Like YouTube itself, the results you see will reflect the effort you put in.

What's Changed Since 2025 (and Why Old Advice Fails)

If you've looked up YouTube advice before, you may have noticed something frustrating: a lot of it no longer works the way it used to.

Since 2025, YouTube has continued to shift away from surface-level metrics like subscribers, tags, and viral tricks. The platform now prioritizes viewer behavior: what people actually watch, how long they stay, and whether they come back. Discovery is driven less by hacks and more by clarity, consistency, and audience satisfaction.

Shorts have also become a core part of growth rather than an optional feature, while monetization has expanded far beyond ads alone. At the same time, new tools (including AI-assisted creation) have changed how creators plan, produce, and refine content.

In the early days of YouTube, creators often talked about "beating the algorithm" as if it were a gatekeeper or a puzzle to be solved. However, it is more helpful to view the algorithm not as a person or a hurdle, but as a highly sophisticated matchmaker. Its entire job is to look at the millions of videos being uploaded and ask one question: "Which video will this specific viewer enjoy right now?" Instead of pushing your video out to a random crowd, the system "pulls" your content toward people whose past behavior, like what they've watched, liked, or searched for, suggests they will find your work valuable.

Advice that focuses only on beating this system often leads to burnout because it encourages you to chase trends rather than build a real connection with people. When you understand that the algorithm is simply following the audience, you can stop worrying about technical hacks and start focusing on the only thing that truly matters: creating content that satisfies a human being.

That's why *YouTube Success in 30 Days* doesn't rely on outdated tactics or quick wins. Instead, it focuses on systems that align with how YouTube works now so you can build momentum in a way that's realistic, sustainable, and adaptable as the platform continues to evolve.

This book is designed to guide you through that process step-by-step, without overwhelming you. Over the next thirty days, you'll build a strong foundation for your channel. You'll learn how to set things up properly, understand how YouTube actually recommends content today, plan and create videos that people want to watch, and explore realistic ways to earn from your content over time.

This is not about rushing or trying to **blow up** overnight. In 2026, growth on YouTube is about consistency, clarity, and creating content that serves a real audience. Some readers will move through this guide in thirty days.

Others might take longer, and that's perfectly fine. This challenge is flexible by design. Progress matters more than speed.

If you've never filmed a video before, don't know what your channel should be about yet, or feel unsure on camera, you're not behind. This book is built for beginners, with clear explanations and practical steps that make it easy to follow, even if you're completely new to YouTube. You won't be asked to guess or figure things out alone.

We'll focus on building systems that work for you at your pace, in your style, and on your terms.

How to Use This Book

This guide follows a thirty-day structure, with each day covering one key step in building and growing your YouTube channel. From your first idea to publishing and beyond, you'll have guidance at every stage: setup, planning, filming, editing, growth strategies, monetization options, and sustainability.

You can follow it day by day or move more slowly if needed. Think of this as a supportive roadmap rather than a strict schedule. Life happens, and YouTube should complement your life, not compete with it.

Here's some of what you'll learn along the way:

- How to set up your channel with today's best practices.
- What equipment and tools actually matter in 2026.
- How to plan, film, and edit content efficiently.
- How to grow an audience without relying on luck or trends.
- Different ways creators earn income on YouTube.
- How to build a channel that can last long-term.

Each day includes a short explanation of what to focus on, followed by clear, actionable steps. There's no technical overload and no confusing jargon, just practical guidance you can apply immediately.

You'll also benefit from real-world creator insights, helping you avoid common mistakes and move forward with confidence as the platform continues to evolve.

What You'll Need to Get Started

To begin this challenge, you'll need:

- A device with internet access (phone, tablet, laptop, or computer).
- A Google account to create your YouTube channel.
- About thirty to sixty minutes a day, or whatever time you can realistically commit.
- A quiet space for planning, learning, and optional recording.
- A willingness to learn, experiment, and keep going, even when things feel unfamiliar.

What you don't need is perfect gear, a flawless plan, or instant results. You don't need to be confident on camera from day one. This is about starting where you are and improving as you go.

YouTube rewards creators who are consistent, thoughtful, and willing to adapt. You don't need to chase virality to succeed. You need a clear system, and that's exactly what this book is here to help you build.

When you're ready, turn the page.

Day 1 starts now.

Week 1: Understanding the Platform

Every successful YouTube channel begins with a solid foundation, and that's the focus of this first week.

In Week 1, you'll set up the essentials that support everything that comes next. You'll create and organize your accounts, choose a channel name with intention, and learn how YouTube works in 2026 (from how content gets discovered to how creators build visibility over time). You'll also explore how branding and monetization fit into your overall strategy, even at the very beginning.

This week is about gaining clarity. You'll start defining your niche, understanding who your content is for, and mapping out your first video ideas with purpose instead of guesswork.

Whether your goal is creative expression, audience growth, income, or a mix of all three, Week 1 gives you the structure and direction you need to move forward with confidence. This is where your creator journey truly takes shape.

Day 1: Why YouTube in 2026? Opportunities, Myths, and Reality

Starting something new often comes with the feeling that you're already behind. It can look like everyone else has figured it out, built an audience, or claimed their space. But if you're here right now, you're not late; you're arriving at a moment when YouTube is more open and flexible than it's ever been.

YouTube in 2026 isn't about jumping on trends as fast as possible or competing with celebrities. It's about visibility, discovery, and building trust over time. The platform has evolved into a place where creators grow through consistency and clarity, not perfection. New voices appear every day, and many of them start with far less than you might expect. This shift has changed what success looks like.

In the past, advice focused on chasing viral moments, obsessing over subscribers, or trying to **beat** the algorithm. Now, YouTube rewards creators who understand their audience, keep viewers engaged, and show up consistently with a clear direction. Growth is less about luck and more about building a system that works with the platform instead of against it. And yes, YouTube is still one of the strongest long-term ways to earn online.

The YouTube Landscape (By the Numbers)

To understand why YouTube is still worth starting in 2026, it helps to look at the bigger picture. As of 2025, over 618,000 YouTube channels worldwide have reached at least 100,000 subscribers, and nearly 70,000 channels have crossed the one-million-subscriber mark. Thousands of creators have built audiences large enough to support full-time careers, and many more are growing smaller, highly profitable channels without ever becoming famous.

In the U.S. alone, more than 100,000 channels have earned YouTube Play Button awards, while countries like India, Brazil, Indonesia, and Japan continue to see massive creator growth. This tells us something important: YouTube success isn't limited to one niche, one country, or one type of creator.

At the same time, only a tiny fraction of channels reach the very top levels of the platform. Fewer than 3,000 channels worldwide have over 10 million subscribers, and only a handful have crossed the 100 million mark. That gap isn't meant to discourage you; it's meant to clarify expectations. Sustainable success on YouTube doesn't come from chasing extremes. It comes from building a clear audience, delivering consistent value, and growing steadily over time. In other words, YouTube isn't **too crowded**. It's segmented. And that's exactly why new creators still have room to grow.

Creators today make money through ads, brand partnerships, affiliate marketing, digital products, memberships, and more. But beyond income, YouTube can also help you build a personal brand, open doors to new opportunities, and create work that compounds over time. One video can continue bringing value (views, income, and connections) long after it's published.

A common myth is that you need expensive gear or a massive personality to succeed. In reality, many thriving channels are built with simple setups, clear ideas, and a willingness to improve over time. You don't need to look or sound perfect. You need to be understandable, consistent, and intentional. This guide exists to help you approach YouTube realistically, not as a gamble, but as a skill you can learn.

Over the next thirty days, you'll move from idea to action. You'll set up your channel properly, understand how YouTube actually makes decisions, create your first content with confidence, and lay the groundwork for growth. You don't need to have everything figured out today. You just need to take the first step. And that starts here.

Your Action Steps for Today

1. Clarify your reason for starting. Take five to ten minutes to write down *why* you want to start a YouTube channel. Is it to share knowledge, express creativity, build a brand, earn income, or explore a new direction? Your reason doesn't need to sound impressive, it just needs to be honest. This will guide your decisions later.

2. Notice what draws you in as a viewer. Write down three to five YouTube channels you enjoy watching. Pay attention to what keeps you coming back. Is it the tone, the topic, the storytelling, or the way the creator explains things? This isn't about copying; it's about recognizing what resonates with you.

Optional Reflection

Imagine your channel one year from now. What kind of content are you creating? How does it feel to know you followed through instead of putting it off? Let yourself picture it without worrying about the details yet.

There's no pressure to get everything right today. Progress on YouTube comes from showing up, learning, and adjusting as you go. Today is about intention, not execution.

When you're ready, move on to Day 2. Next, we'll break down how **YouTube's ecosystem actually works**, and how to think like a creator from the start.

Day 2: The YouTube Ecosystem in 2026 and How Discovery Really Works

Now that you've clarified why you want to start a YouTube channel, it's time to understand the environment you're stepping into. Not just what YouTube is, but how it functions as a platform in 2026, and why that matters for new creators.

YouTube today is less of a social network and more of a global discovery engine. With a reach of approximately 2.85 billion users worldwide, it is the second-largest search engine on the internet, surpassed only by Google. People don't come to YouTube casually; they come with intent. They search for explanations, tutorials, reviews, entertainment, inspiration, and solutions to specific problems. This is a critical shift to understand.

Viewers aren't just **watching videos**. They're actively **looking for value.** That's why YouTube continues to compete directly with streaming services, podcasts, and traditional television (especially as more people watch content on smart TVs rather than phones).

At the same time, YouTube operates on a truly global scale. India alone has nearly 500 million YouTube users, making it the largest market on the platform. The U.S. follows with roughly 250 million users, and then the numbers spread across other countries and continents. This tells us something important: YouTube is not a niche platform, and it's not limited to one region, language, or type of creator. It's a worldwide system of audiences, many of whom are underserved and still looking for content that speaks directly to them.

Videos succeed because they answer specific questions, meet clear needs, or hold attention within defined communities. That means your goal isn't to appeal to everyone. It's to reach the right viewers. This is where many beginners get stuck.

They see billions of users and millions of creators and assume success requires being louder, flashier, or trendier than everyone else. In reality, YouTube favors creators who understand how discovery works and who create content with intention. Long-form videos build depth and trust. Shorts introduce new viewers to your channel. Community tools help strengthen relationships. Together, these formats form an ecosystem, not isolated tactics.

It's also worth noting that YouTube is deeply integrated into the **digital economy**. Brands actively use the platform to advertise, collaborate with creators, and analyze performance data. This means YouTube isn't just a creative outlet; it's a serious business environment. Even small channels can attract opportunities when their content is focused and their audience is clear.

The takeaway for today is simple: You don't need to be perfect, viral, or universally appealing. You need to understand the landscape you're entering and position yourself thoughtfully within it. That understanding starts now.

Your Action Steps for Today

1. Watch YouTube with creator awareness. Choose two or three creators you enjoy, large or small, and watch their videos intentionally. Pay attention to:

- How they open their videos.
- How their titles and thumbnails set expectations.
- How the content is structured.
- What viewers respond to in the comments.

Take brief notes and learn how each creator communicates clearly with their audience.

2. Explore your potential niche. Search YouTube for topics you'd like to make videos about. Watch a few of the top results and ask yourself:

- What problem or question is this video addressing?
- Why might viewers be clicking on it?
- Is there something you could explain differently, more clearly, or from another perspective?

You're not looking for gaps to exploit; you're looking for conversations you could genuinely contribute to. Don't choose a topic simply because you've heard someone say it makes a lot of money. Choose something you could talk about for hours without getting bored, something you'd still want to create videos about even if you weren't getting paid for it. The best long-term channels are built on curiosity, passion, and genuine interest, not just profit.

Optional Reflection

Where do you see space for your voice? What perspective, experience, or approach could you bring that feels natural to you?

There's no pressure to decide everything today. Awareness comes before action.

Tomorrow, we'll move from observation to execution as you begin **setting up your YouTube account properly**, so when you start publishing, you're building on a solid foundation.

Day 3: Setting Up Your Google & YouTube Accounts the Right Way

Today is where your YouTube journey becomes tangible. Not an idea, not a plan, but an actual presence on the platform. By the end of this day, you won't just be thinking about becoming a creator; you'll have officially claimed your space on YouTube.

Before any videos are filmed or ideas are refined, YouTube requires one essential thing: a properly set-up account. This step may feel simple, but it's foundational. Getting it right now ensures everything else (uploads, analytics, monetization, and future growth) works smoothly later. Your channel, analytics, monetization, copyright tools, and even visibility are all managed through this system. Setting things up intentionally from the start gives you more flexibility as your channel grows.

Step 1: Your Google Account (The Backbone of Your Channel)

Every YouTube channel is powered by a Google account. If you already have one, you can use it. If not, creating one takes only a few minutes.

Some creators prefer to use their personal Google account. Others prefer creating a separate one specifically for YouTube, especially if they plan to treat their channel as a business or long-term project. Either option works. What matters is choosing the setup that feels easiest to manage.

This Google account will later connect to:

- YouTube Studio.
- Channel analytics.
- Monetization tools like **AdSense**.
- Copyright and content management features.

Think of it as the control hub behind everything you'll do as a creator.

Step 2: Creating Your YouTube Channel

Once you're signed into Google, creating a YouTube channel is straightforward.

1. Go to YouTube and sign in.
2. Click your profile icon in the top-right corner.
3. Select **Create a channel.**
4. Enter a channel name and add a profile image (both can be changed later).

That's it. Your channel now exists.

At this stage, you're not trying to make anything perfect. You're simply establishing the account so YouTube recognizes you as a creator. We'll refine names, visuals, and positioning later.

A Quick Note on Multiple Channels

As of 2026, YouTube allows one Google account to own multiple channels using what's called a **Brand Account**. Many creators use this feature to manage different projects without juggling logins. If you ever want to expand, this option will be available to you.

Step 3: Getting Familiar with YouTube Studio

After your channel is created, head to **YouTube Studio**. This is where everything happens behind the scenes. You can access it by clicking your profile icon in the top-right corner of YouTube and selecting **YouTube Studio**, or by going directly to **studio.youtube.com**.

Inside YouTube Studio, you'll be able to:

- Upload and manage videos.
- Check performance and audience data.
- Customize your channel.
- Access monetization tools.
- Manage comments and community features.

For today, you don't need to understand every section. Just click around. Familiarity now will save you frustration later.

Step 4: Enable Key Features Early

Before you start uploading seriously, there's one important step worth doing now: **verifying your phone number.**

This verification unlocks essential features that most creators use, such as uploading videos longer than fifteen minutes, adding custom thumbnails, going live, and accessing additional account protections. Doing this early prevents unnecessary limitations later on.

To verify your phone number, open **YouTube Studio**, click **Settings** in the left-hand menu, then select **Channel** and go to **Feature Eligibility**. Under the section for intermediate features, click **Verify Phone Number** and follow the on-screen instructions. You'll receive a code by text or call, which you'll need to enter to complete the process.

The entire step takes just a few minutes, and once it's done, your account will be ready for all standard creator features.

A Note on Privacy and Control

Everything you upload starts private, and you decide when it becomes public.

YouTube gives you full control over visibility settings. Videos can be set to **Private**, **Unlisted**, or **Public**. You can experiment, test uploads, or prepare content without anyone seeing it. There's no pressure to publish before you're ready.

This is your space. You decide when and how it's seen. (We will learn more about this on *Day 20: What to Check Before Publishing*).

Your Action Steps for Today

1. **Create your YouTube channel.** Sign in, set it up, and make it official. Even if nothing is uploaded yet, today is about claiming your channel.

2. **Open YouTube Studio.** Spend a few minutes exploring the dashboard, content tab, and settings. You don't need to memorize anything; just get comfortable.

3. Verify your account. Enable key features now so you don't run into limitations later.

Optional Reflection

How did it feel to create your channel? Excited? Nervous? Both? Jot down a few thoughts. Starting something meaningful often feels uncomfortable, and that's usually a good sign.

Tomorrow, we'll begin shaping your identity as a creator by focusing on **channel direction and naming strategy**, so everything you build going forward feels intentional.

You're officially in.

Day 4: Choosing Your Direction: Niche, Audience, and Creative Intent

Before you worry about channel names, visuals, or branding, there's one decision that shapes everything else you'll do on YouTube: **direction**. What kind of content are you creating, and who is it meant for?

This is the stage where many creators either rush ahead without a plan or get paralyzed by the fear of making the wrong choice. Both paths lead to the same destination: a channel full of scattered videos, inconsistent growth, and constant second-guessing.

Taking the time to define your focus today isn't about boxing yourself in or limiting your creativity; it's about giving your channel **momentum**. When you know exactly who you are talking to and what value you are providing, every decision, from your titles to your filming style, becomes faster and more effective. By narrowing your lens now, you aren't closing doors; you're building a clear path for your audience to find you.

YouTube today is built around **intent**. Viewers arrive looking for something specific (answers, entertainment, guidance, or connection). The algorithm pays close attention to who clicks, who stays, and who returns. When your content consistently serves a clear type of viewer, YouTube understands where to place it. That's why channels that grow steadily tend to share two traits:

- A recognizable content direction.
- A clear understanding of their audience.

This doesn't mean locking yourself into one idea forever. It means choosing a **starting lane** that both people and the platform can recognize.

Understanding Niches Beyond "What It's About"

A niche isn't just a topic. It's the **context** in which your content creates value. For example:

- "Fitness" is broad.
- "Beginner home workouts for busy parents" is focused.

- "Low-Impact Workouts for People Restarting Their Fitness Journey" is intentional.

In 2026, niches are closely tied to **viewer intent** and **advertiser demand**. Viewer intent simply means what your audience is actively looking for or trying to achieve when they watch your videos, for example, learning a skill, solving a problem, or making a purchase decision. Advertiser demand refers to how valuable that audience is to advertisers and how many brands want to show ads to those viewers. One way YouTube reflects this is through your video's **CPM** (Cost Per Mille), which is the amount advertisers are willing to pay for every 1,000 ad views.

Here's the simple distinction:

- **CPM** shows how much advertisers are willing to pay to show ads to an audience.
- **RPM** (Revenue Per Mille) shows how much you, the creator, actually earn after YouTube takes its share.

Higher CPM niches usually involve decision-making: money, learning, buying, or long-term improvement. That's why education, technology, personal finance, and automotive content tend to earn more per view than pure entertainment, even with fewer views. This doesn't mean you should chase the highest-paying niche. It means you should understand that **profitability on YouTube comes from alignment**, not volume alone. Some niches grow through scale (like entertainment or gaming). Others grow through value and trust (like education, finance, wellness, or tech). Both can work, if they fit you.

Popular YouTube Niches in 2026 (And Why They Work)

Rather than thinking in terms of **best** or **worst**, it helps to see how different niches succeed:

- **Education & Tutorials:** These videos teach something useful (like study tips, writing help, or software guides). They often earn well because viewers are actively trying to learn.

- **Technology Reviews:** Channels that review phones, laptops, or gadgets. They can earn more because viewers are often planning to buy something.
- **Personal Finance & Investing:** Videos about saving money, budgeting, or investing. These can earn high income even with fewer views, because advertisers pay more to reach this audience.
- **Beauty & Fashion:** Channels focused on makeup, skincare, and style. Creators often earn by recommending or partnering with brands that sell products.
- **Gaming:** Gameplay, reviews, and live streams. These channels grow through loyal audiences who watch for longer periods of time.
- **Entertainment & Comedy:** Skits, storytelling, or humor. These channels rely on getting lots of views and sharing to grow.
- **Health, Wellness & Mental Health:** Videos about fitness, self-care, or emotional wellbeing. These build strong trust with viewers and grow steadily over time.
- **Food & Cooking:** Recipes, kitchen tips, and cooking challenges. These do well because food is something everyone searches for.
- **Motivation & Self-Improvement:** Videos that help viewers improve their habits, mindset, or productivity. Many creators earn by selling courses, books, or coaching.
- **DIY, Crafts & Home Projects:** Tutorials on building, fixing, or creating things. These videos keep getting views for years because people are always searching for them.
- **Parenting & Family:** Content for parents, families, or children. These channels grow through strong viewer loyalty and often attract family-focused advertisers.
- **Pets & Animals:** Fun or educational pet videos. These grow through emotional sharing and sponsorships.
- **Automotive:** Reviews or tutorials about cars and bikes. These can earn well because car-related audiences are valuable to advertisers.

None of these are **easy**. All of them work when the creator understands their audience and delivers consistently. You don't have to squeeze yourself into a rigid category to succeed on YouTube. Many strong channels blend formats, tones, and ideas. What matters most is that viewers quickly understand why your content exists and what kind of value they'll get from it. You don't need to be the world's top expert, either. In fact, it's often easier to learn from someone who's only a few steps ahead of you. They still remember what it was like to be stuck, which questions felt confusing, and how to solve problems in a simple, practical way. Someone who's 100 steps ahead may be highly skilled, but they can forget the small details beginners struggle with.

Some of the most compelling creators simply speak from experience, curiosity, or a willingness to explain things honestly. If you're unsure where to start, ask yourself:

- What subjects can I talk about without getting bored?
- What experiences or challenges have taught me something useful?
- What do people naturally ask me about or trust me to explain?
- What kind of content do I already enjoy watching and could imagine creating consistently?

Often, your strongest direction lives at the intersection of **interest, experience, and usefulness**. And yes, YouTube truly does have room for ideas that might seem unusual at first.

A great example is **Ask a Mortician**, a channel with nearly two million subscribers built around a topic many creators would avoid entirely. Instead of shying away from death, funerals, and mourning, a licensed mortician answers questions people are curious about but rarely feel comfortable asking. Topics range from the practical to the unexpected (what happens during cremation, whether certain burial products are necessary, or how different cultures approach death).

The success of channels like this isn't accidental. They work because they serve a specific audience with clarity, honesty, and purpose. They don't try to appeal to everyone. They speak directly to the people who are already searching for those answers. **That's the real takeaway:** If you're willing to show up consistently and create content with intention, there's likely an audience looking for exactly what you have to offer, even if it feels niche, unconventional, or oddly specific. Your job isn't to chase what's popular. It's to choose a direction you can commit to and communicate it clearly.

Niche Research: Validating Your Direction

Before you record a single frame, you need to validate your niche. In 2026, successful creators don't guess what people want; they research what is already working. The goal is to find the **Visual Language** of your specific category.

1. The Research Process

Search for your potential niche on YouTube and look at the top-performing videos from the last six months. Don't just look at the view counts; look at the **patterns**.

- **Identify High Performers:** Look for videos that have more views than the channel has subscribers. This is a sign that the topic itself is driving growth, not just an existing fan base. For example, if a channel has 2,000 subscribers but one video has 150,000 views, that video likely reached a much wider audience through search, recommendations, or suggested videos. That is a strong signal that the topic resonates and has significant growth potential, suggesting you should consider using that subject or format in future uploads
- **Study the Visual Language:** Every niche has a set of cues that tell the viewer, "This is for you"
    - In **Finance**, it might be clean white backgrounds, minimal figures, and text.
    - In **Gaming**, it might be high-saturation colors and **reaction** faces.
    - In **Education**, it might be a split screen showing a **Before/After** or a specific diagram style.
- **Look for Format Consistency:** Do the top videos in your niche use voice-overs or face-to-camera talking head shots?

A **voice-over** means the creator is speaking while other footage plays on screen. This footage is called **B-roll**, and it can include screen recordings, images, clips, animations, or examples that support what's being said. The creator's face may not appear at all. A **face-to-camera** (or "talking head") video shows the creator speaking directly to the camera, usually explaining or teaching something while being visible on screen. In these videos, B-roll is often added later to show examples, demonstrate steps, or keep the video visually engaging. Pay attention to which style appears most often among high-performing videos. That pattern can help you decide what format is easier and more realistic for you to start with.

2. Speaking the Language

Understanding these patterns isn't about copying; it's about **fluency**. When you use the colors, fonts, and pacing that your audience already recognizes, you lower the barrier to entry. You are signaling to both the viewer and the algorithm that you belong in this club. Niche research should be done **before** launching. By identifying the visual and verbal language of your category now, you can design your very first video to feel like it belongs alongside the best in the business.

The Goal: Familiar but Different

Once you have identified the patterns and **Visual Language** of your niche, it's time to find your place within it. The secret to a successful launch isn't reinventing the wheel; it's mastering the balance between **recognition** and **novelty**.

The goal is to be familiar and different at the same time.

- **Familiar enough** that viewers recognize the niche instantly. When a viewer sees your video, they should immediately know if it's a tech review, a cooking tutorial, or a personal vlog. This lowers the **mental friction** for the viewer and helps the algorithm categorize your video correctly.
- **Different enough** that your video feels fresh and worth clicking. Once they know what it is, they need a reason to choose yours. This is where your unique perspective, your specific personality, or your **one adjustment** comes in.

By researching first, you ensure you aren't so different that the audience (and the algorithm) is confused. By being unique, you ensure you aren't so familiar that you become invisible. Use research to build the foundation of your house, but use your personal intent to choose the color of the door. Research tells you how to be relevant; your voice tells you how to be memorable.

Now Let's Talk About Audience

Once you choose a direction, the next question becomes, "Who is this for?" You don't need a marketing persona; you need **clarity**. Ask yourself:

- Are they beginners or experienced in this field?
- What problem are they trying to solve?
- What level of detail do they need?
- What tone would feel natural and trustworthy to them?

A clear audience makes everything else easier (video ideas, titles, descriptions, and thumbnails), and even how you speak on camera. If you're unsure, think backward. Was there a time when you were struggling with something your niche covers? What kind of content would have helped you then? That version of you is often your first audience.

Why Choosing a Niche and Audience are Important

In 2026, YouTube functions less like a filing cabinet and more like a high-speed **matchmaker**. It doesn't find viewers for your videos; it finds the right videos for its viewers. This is the biggest reason why choosing a direction (or **niche**) matters. To grow, you don't just need to be **searchable**, you need to be **recommendable**. Most views today come from **Home**, **Suggested**, and **Browse** feeds. For your video to appear there, the algorithm needs to know exactly which club or interest group you belong to.

Why Genres Matter for Discovery

Because the system is a matchmaker, it looks for **topic clusters,** which are groups of similar videos that people tend to watch together.

- **The Genre Signal:** Every type of video has a specific **vibe**, the way it's edited, the music used, and how fast the creator talks. If you make a "Day in the Life" video that looks and feels like other popular ones, the algorithm thinks: "Aha! This belongs in the 'Vlog' category. I'll show it to people who already enjoy vlogs." By using familiar styles, you're helping YouTube categorize you faster.

- **People over Pixels (Affinity Scoring):** In the past, we focused on **keywords** and tags. Today, YouTube cares more about **who** is watching. The system looks for **Affinity**, which is just a fancy way of saying **shared interests**. It tries to match your video with people who already love specific things, like **minimalist tech** or **urban gardening**. If your video appeals to that specific group of people, YouTube will keep showing it to more people just like them.

The Testing Phase

You don't need a huge audience to get started. When you upload a video, YouTube uses an **initial test group** strategy. It shows your video to a small group of people who have watched similar topics.

- **If they click and stay:** YouTube expands the circle to a larger group.
- **If they skip:** The system assumes the **match** was wrong and stops circulating the video.

You aren't competing against a search bar. You are competing for a spot in a viewer's personalized feed. Choosing a niche is simply giving the algorithm a clear map so it knows exactly where to deliver your content.

Your Action Steps for Today

1. Choose your starting direction. Write down the main topic your channel will focus on for the next five to ten videos. It should feel focused but flexible.

2. Define your ideal viewer. In a few sentences, describe who you're creating for. Be specific enough to guide your decisions, but don't overthink it.

3. Do a quick reality check on YouTube. Search for your topic. Look at a few top results. Notice formats, titles, and viewer questions. Ask yourself where you could add clarity, personality, or a different perspective.

4. Read the comments. Comments reveal intent. What are people confused about? What do they ask repeatedly? These are future video ideas waiting to happen.

Optional Reflection

How does choosing a clear niche and audience change how you think about your channel? Does it make your next steps feel more manageable?

Tomorrow, we'll build directly on this work as we move into **channel names, positioning, and branding,** using your direction and audience as the foundation.

Day 5: Naming, First Impressions, and Channel Identity

Your channel name is often the first thing people notice, sometimes before they ever see your face or watch a video. Along with your profile photo and description, it sets expectations and helps viewers quickly decide whether your channel feels relevant to them. Today is about choosing a clear, workable identity for your channel. Not a final version; just a strong starting point that aligns with the niche and audience you defined yesterday.

Why Channel Identity Matters

In 2026, people discover channels across search results, Shorts feeds, TV home screens, recommendations, and external links. Your channel name, profile image, and description often appear together in these spaces. That means your identity should:

- Be easy to recognize.
- Feel intentional and trustworthy.
- Communicate what your channel is about at a glance.

YouTube allows you to change these elements later, especially early on. Still, starting with clarity makes growth smoother and helps YouTube understand how to position your content.

Choosing a Strong Channel Name

There's no single **perfect** name, but effective channel names tend to share a few traits:

1. Simple and memorable. If someone hears your channel name once, they should be able to find it again easily. Avoid extra numbers, unusual spelling, or symbols that make your name harder to search.

2. Aligned with your content.

Your name doesn't need to include keywords, but it should hint at what viewers can expect, especially while your channel is new. Many successful creators use descriptive names that instantly show their niche, like **Linus Tech Tips** (technology), **Yoga With Adriene** (fitness), or **CrashCourse** (education). The goal is simple: when someone sees your channel name, they should have a rough idea of what to expect from your content.

3. Distinct. Before settling on a name, search it on YouTube and Google. If it's already widely used or closely associated with another creator or brand, it may be harder to stand out.

4. Flexible. If your content may evolve, choose a name that gives you room to grow rather than locking you into one narrow idea.

5. Free of trademarked or restricted terms. Avoid using **YouTube**, **brand names**, or anything you don't own the rights to.

You can use your real name, a variation of it, a descriptive phrase, or something original. What matters most is that it feels natural for you to say, write, and build around. If you're feeling stuck, this is a great place to use AI as a brainstorming partner. You can open ChatGPT and try a prompt like:

"Give me 10 YouTube channel name ideas for a channel about [your topic]. Make them sound clear, modern, and easy to remember. Please keep the channel name in tune with the tone of my channel, which is [add your tone, i.e., academic/informative/funny]."

Then refine it further:

"Now make them more creative and unique, but still straightforward enough to reflect the essence of my channel."

You don't have to pick the perfect name right away; just choose something you feel comfortable with for now. You can always evolve your brand as your channel grows.

Your Channel Description

Your channel description helps viewers, and YouTube, understand what your content is about. At this stage, it doesn't need to be long or optimized; it's best to keep it simple. A good starting description:

- Explains who the channel is for.
- Describes what kind of content you'll share.
- Sounds human and approachable.

One or two clear sentences are enough for now. You'll revisit and refine this later as your content develops.

Profile Photo: A Clear, Recognizable Signal

Your profile photo appears everywhere, next to your videos, in comments, and across recommendations. Its job is recognition, not perfection. For now:

- Use a clear photo of your face **or** a simple logo.
- Make sure it's easy to see at small sizes.
- Avoid clutter or overly detailed images.

If you don't have a photo or logo yet, tools like ChatGPT can help you generate simple logo ideas or prompts you can use with image generators. You can always refine or replace it later.

Channel Banners and Video Watermarks: What They Are and How to Add Them

As your channel starts to take shape, YouTube gives you a couple of simple visual tools that help reinforce your identity: **channel banners** and **video watermarks**. These aren't required to start uploading, but they're useful once you want your channel to look more complete and recognizable.

Channel Banner

Your channel banner is the wide image that appears at the top of your channel homepage, especially noticeable on desktop and TV screens. In 2026, more viewers are discovering channels on TVs, which makes banners more visible than ever. A good banner:

- Communicates what your channel is about at a glance.
- Feels consistent with your tone or niche.

- Doesn't need to be overly detailed or polished.

You can keep it simple; bold text, a colored background, or a minimal design is enough to start.

Video Watermark

A video watermark is a small image that appears in the bottom-right corner of your videos. When viewers hover over it, they're prompted to subscribe. Think of it as a subtle reminder rather than a sales pitch. Most creators use:

- Their logo.
- Their channel initials.
- A simple icon or symbol.

Like everything else, this can be updated later.

Important Reminder

You do **not** need a banner or watermark before you start posting videos. If designing visuals feels overwhelming right now, skip this step and come back later. Content comes first. Branding supports it, not the other way around. As your channel grows, these elements help reinforce recognition and professionalism, but they're tools, not prerequisites. When you are ready to create them, you can make both your banner and watermark for free using beginner-friendly tools like **Canva**, **Adobe Express**, or **Pixlr**. Canva is especially helpful because it includes ready-made **YouTube banner and watermark templates in the exact recommended sizes**, so you don't have to worry about dimensions or formatting.

How to Update Your Channel Name, Description, Banner, and Watermark

All of your channel's core details are managed inside **YouTube Studio**. You can update these settings at any time, and nothing is permanent (many creators adjust them as their channel evolves).

Step-by-Step: Where to Make Changes

1. Open **YouTube Studio.**
    - Click on your profile icon on YouTube and select **YouTube Studio**, or
    - Go directly to **studio.youtube.com**
2. In the left-hand menu, click on **Customization.**
3. You'll see three main tabs:
    - **Basic Info**, where you can edit your channel name and description.
    - **Branding**, where you can upload or change your profile photo, channel banner, and video watermark.
    - **Layout**, where you can control how your channel homepage is organized.

What You Can Update Here

- **Channel name:** Adjust or refine your name at any time.

- **Channel description:** Rewrite or expand it as your content becomes clearer.
- **Profile photo**: Upload or replace your image for better recognition.
- **Channel banner**: Add or update the large image shown at the top of your channel.
- **Video watermark**: Add a small image that appears on your videos and prompts viewers to subscribe.

To add or change your **banner** or **watermark**, select the **Branding** tab and upload the images where prompted. YouTube will show you previews so you can see how everything looks across different devices. After making any changes, click **Publish** in the top-right corner to save them.

Branding Comes After Clarity

It is very common for new creators to spend days agonizing over the perfect shade of blue for their banner or the exact font for their channel banner. While those things are fun, it is important to remember that your **branding** is actually much deeper than just your colors. Once you have your name, description, and profile photo in place, the rest of your branding will start to feel much more natural.

In the world of YouTube, branding is the **overall feeling** someone gets when they interact with your channel. Think of it as the **personality** of your digital home. It includes things like:

- **Your Tone and Personality:** Are you a high-energy teacher or a calm, comforting mentor?
- **The Content You Create:** What is the specific **flavor** of your videos?
- **The Problems You Solve:** What is the one thing your viewers know they can count on you for?
- **The Experience:** How do viewers feel the moment they land on your page? Do they feel inspired, informed, or entertained?

The most important thing to know is that **you don't need a final look today.** You don't need a professional logo or a custom-designed banner to start. Instead, just start noticing what style, mood, or energy feels most natural for you.

As you film your first few videos, you will naturally discover your voice. You might find you prefer a **dark and moody** cinematic look or a **bright and airy** educational vibe. **Visual polish can always be added later; finding your direction must come first.** By focusing on your message and your audience first, your visual brand will eventually build itself around the real you.

Your Action Steps for Today

1. Brainstorm channel names. Write down five to ten possible names. Don't judge them yet; get everything out of your head and onto paper. If you need inspiration, you can use tools like ChatGPT to generate ideas based on your niche, tone, or audience.

2. Check name availability. Search your top ideas on YouTube and Google to see what already exists. If you're thinking long-term, you may also want to see whether a matching website domain or social media handle is available. This step isn't required, but it can be helpful if you plan to build a brand beyond YouTube. You can use websites like **Namecheckly** that check the availability of both **domain names and social usernames** side-by-side.

3. Choose a working name. Pick one name to move forward with for now. You can always change it later; momentum matters more than certainty.

4. Add a profile photo and short description. Upload a simple profile image and write a brief channel description. Keep it clear, not perfect.

Optional Reflection

Does your channel identity feel aligned with the kind of content and audience you want to grow? Does it feel like something you'd be comfortable building on?

Tomorrow, we'll shift into **how YouTube monetization actually works;** what's realistic, what's changed, and how creators earn over time.

You're building this step by step, and it's starting to take shape.

Day 6: How YouTube Monetization Works (What to Aim For and Why)

As your channel begins to take shape, it's natural to start wondering how creators actually make money on YouTube. Monetization is one of the biggest motivators, but it's also one of the most misunderstood parts of the platform. The first thing to know is this: **YouTube monetization is not a single switch you flip.** It's a collection of features that become available as your channel grows, proves itself, and stays in good standing. Understanding how this system works early helps you set realistic goals and avoid frustration later.

What Monetization Really Means on YouTube

In 2026, earning money on YouTube happens through a mix of tools and revenue streams, not just ads. Most of these features become available after your channel is accepted into the **YouTube Partner Program (YPP)**. Before approval, YouTube evaluates your channel as a whole. This includes:

- The originality of your content.
- Whether your videos follow advertiser-friendly guidelines.
- Your compliance with copyright rules.
- Your overall channel activity and consistency.

Approval is not automatic, even if you hit the numbers. YouTube manually reviews channels to ensure they meet platform standards.

Ways Creators Earn Money After Approval

Once your channel is accepted into the **YPP**, you may earn income through several paths, depending on your content style and audience:

- **Ad revenue** from ads shown on long-form videos and live streams.
- **YouTube Premium revenue**, which pays you when Premium subscribers watch your content.

- **Fan funding tools**, such as Super Chat, Super Stickers, and Super Thanks.
- **YouTube Shopping and affiliate features**, allowing you to tag products directly in videos or posts.
- **Brand deals and paid partnerships**, which happen outside YouTube but rely on an active, monetized channel.

Not every channel uses all of these. Monetization works best when it aligns with your format, whether that's long-form videos, Shorts, live streams, or a combination. (All of these are detailed on *Day 25: Monetization Models That Scale*).

To put the scale in perspective: between **2021 and 2023, YouTube paid over $70 billion to creators and media companies**. That money didn't go only to massive channels; it flowed across many different content types.

YouTube Monetization Requirements

To apply for the **YouTube Partner Program**, your channel must meet **all** of the following conditions:

- At least **1,000 subscribers.**
- One of these activity thresholds:
  - **4,000 valid public watch hours** in the last twelve months (long-form videos and live streams), **or**
  - **10 million valid public Shorts views** in the last ninety days.
- No active community guideline or copyright strikes.
- Original content that follows advertiser-friendly guidelines.
- A verified Google account with **two-step verification enabled.**
- A connected and approved **Google AdSense account** (covered tomorrow).

YouTube takes policy compliance seriously. In just one quarter of 2024, **millions of videos were removed**, most flagged by automated systems. This is why consistency, originality, and rule-following matter as much as growth (we will talk about this more in Day 21: *Copyright, Fair Use and Monetization Safety*).

Unlocking Early Monetization: The 500-Subscriber Tier

In 2026, you no longer have to wait until you hit the magic number of 1,000 subscribers to start building a business on YouTube. The platform now offers a two-tier system that allows smaller creators to begin earning through **Fan Funding** and **YouTube Shopping** much earlier than before (detailed in *Day 25: Monetization Models that Scale)*. This **Early Access tier** is designed for creators who have built a small but highly engaged community. While it doesn't unlock traditional ad revenue yet, it gives you the tools to turn your most loyal viewers into active supporters.

The Early Access Requirements

To apply for this first level of the **YPP**, your channel needs to meet these specific milestones:

- **500 Subscribers:** Half the requirement of the full program.
- **Three Public Uploads:** You must have published at least three videos in the last ninety days to prove your channel is active.
- **Engagement Milestone (Pick One):**
  - **3,000 Public Watch Hours** on long-form videos in the last twelve months.
  - **3 Million Public Shorts Views** in the last Ninety days.

What You Unlock at 500 Subscribers

Once you are accepted into this tier, you can turn on several powerful revenue streams:

- **Channel Memberships:** Allow fans to join your channel for a monthly fee in exchange for badges, emojis, and exclusive **members-only** content.
- **Super Chat & Super Stickers:** During live streams or premieres, fans can pay to have their messages highlighted in the chat.
- **Super Thanks:** Viewers can **tip** you on individual uploaded videos or Shorts to show their appreciation.
- **YouTube Shopping:** You can link your own store or promote

products directly beneath your videos, creating a **boutique** experience for your audience.

Moving to Full Monetization

The best part of this system is that it's a stepping stone. Once you've joined the program at 500 subscribers, you don't have to re-apply when you reach the next level. As soon as you hit **1,000 subscribers** and either **4,000 public watch hours** or **ten million public Shorts views**, YouTube will automatically unlock **Ad Revenue** for you. This early-access path is perfect for niche creators, like educators, hobbyists, or local community leaders, who may not have millions of views yet but have a dedicated audience ready to support their work. It shifts the focus from **waiting for ads** to **building a community**.

How to Apply for Monetization (When You're Ready)

Once your channel meets the requirements, you'll see progress updates inside YouTube Studio.

To apply:

1. Open **YouTube Studio.**
2. Click on **Earn** (or **Earn money**) in the left-hand menu.
3. Select **Get started** under the **YouTube Partner Program.**
4. Review and accept YouTube's monetization and advertiser-friendly content policies.
5. Connect your Google **AdSense** account.
6. Submit your channel for review.

YouTube's team will review your channel as a whole, not just one video. Approval may take anywhere from a few days to a few weeks, depending on how many applications YouTube is processing at the time and how much content is on your channel for them to review.

As you navigate your new YouTube Studio, you might notice that the **Earn** tab is missing or doesn't look quite like you expected. If you find yourself looking for it without luck, please don't be discouraged. This is a very common part of the journey for beginners, and it usually happens for one of a few specific reasons.

First, it is important to understand that YouTube's monetization features are unlocked as you grow. If you are just starting out, your channel likely hasn't reached the necessary milestones, or **eligibility thresholds**, yet. Think of these as graduation requirements; once you reach a certain number of subscribers and hours of watch time, YouTube will naturally open these doors for you.

Another reason could be your location. While YouTube is a global platform, certain financial features are rolled out region by region. Currently, the **YPP** is available to creators in many parts of the world, including:

- **North and South America**
- **Europe and Asia**
- **Africa and Oceania**

If your country is located within one of these regions, you are in the clear to apply as soon as you meet those subscriber and watch-time goals. If you want to be absolutely sure about your specific country, you can visit the official **YPP** eligibility page. An even easier way is to check the **Earn** tab directly inside your YouTube Studio. Even if you aren't eligible yet, that page will often show your current status and confirm if the program is available in your specific area.

Lastly, the tab might be affected if your account has any specific restrictions or policy issues. This usually happens if there are concerns about the type of content being posted or if certain rules weren't followed. If you feel like you are doing everything right but still don't see your progress, it is always worth checking your channel settings to ensure your account is in good standing.

Remember, every big creator started exactly where you are right now. Seeing that empty **Earn** tab isn't a **no**; it is just a **not yet**.

A Reality Check (and a Reassurance)

Most creators don't start monetizing immediately, and that's normal.

Early success on YouTube comes from building trust, clarity, and consistency. Monetization is a result of that work, not the starting point. Focusing too early on earnings often slows growth rather than speeds it up.

Right now, your job is to understand the system, not rush it.

Your Action Steps for Today

1. Review the monetization requirements. Inside YouTube Studio, explore the **Earn** section (if visible) to see what milestones you're working toward.

2. Set a realistic first goal. Write down a simple target, such as reaching 1,000 subscribers and meeting watch-time requirements within a year. Keep it motivating, not pressuring.

Optional Reflection

What would earning money from YouTube allow you to do creatively, professionally, or personally? Keep that answer in mind as you move forward.

Tomorrow, we'll walk through **setting up Google AdSense**, so you're fully prepared when monetization becomes available. You're learning the system now so it can work for you later.

Day 7: Setting Up Google AdSense

Now that you understand how YouTube monetization works in 2026, it's time to set up the system that actually sends you your money. That system is **Google AdSense**. AdSense is not a bonus feature; it's the payment infrastructure behind YouTube. Even if your channel meets all monetization requirements and is approved for the **YouTube Partner Program (YPP)**, you won't receive earnings without an **AdSense account** connected to your channel.

Think of AdSense as the financial bridge between your videos and your bank account. YouTube calculates what you earn, and AdSense is responsible for holding, verifying, and paying out that money. You don't need to be monetized to set this up, but doing it early removes friction later.

What Google AdSense Does for YouTube Creators

In 2026, Google AdSense handles:

- Ad revenue payouts from long-form videos and live streams.
- YouTube Premium revenue distribution.
- Payments from certain monetization features once enabled.
- Monthly transfers to your bank account.

Once connected, AdSense collects your earnings and releases payments once you reach the minimum payout threshold (usually **$100 USD or the local equivalent**). If you don't reach the threshold in a given month, your balance simply rolls over to the following month.

Before You Create an AdSense Account

Make sure you have the following ready:

- A **Google account** (already set up earlier in this challenge).
- An active **YouTube channel.**
- A **physical mailing address** where you can receive mail.
- A **bank account in your name.**
- Required **tax information** based on your country.

Important to know:

- Each person can only have **one AdSense account.**
- If you've used **AdSense** before (for a website or an older channel), you must use that same account.
- Creating **multiple AdSense accounts** can delay or block payments.

How AdSense Fits Into YouTube Monetization

AdSense alone does not activate monetization; as of today, monetization follows this order:

1. Your channel meets eligibility requirements.
2. You apply and are approved for the **YPP**.
3. Your channel is reviewed for policy compliance.
4. **AdSense is linked** to handle payouts.

Only after all four steps are complete can earnings be paid out.

How to Create Your Google AdSense Account

1. Go to **adsense.google.com.**
2. Sign in with your Google account.
3. Follow the prompts to create your **AdSense** profile.

You'll be asked to enter:

- Your legal name (must match your ID and bank details).
- Your mailing address.
- Your country and currency.
- Your tax information.

Take your time here. Inaccurate details are one of the most common reasons payments get delayed.

Address and Identity Verification

After setup, Google will send a **PIN by mail** to the address you provided. This is a standard security step.

Once the PIN arrives:

- Log in to your **AdSense** account.
- Enter the PIN to confirm your address.

This step can take a couple of weeks depending on where you live. Until it's completed, payments can't be released, so it's best to start early.

Linking AdSense to Your YouTube Channel

When your channel becomes eligible for monetization, YouTube Studio will guide you through linking **AdSense** automatically.

To connect it:

1. Open **YouTube Studio.**
2. Click on **Earn** in the left-hand menu.
3. Select **Get started** under the **YPP**.
4. Sign in to your existing **AdSense** account when prompted.
5. Accept the connection.

Once linked, YouTube and **AdSense** will sync behind the scenes, and you won't need to relink the two for each video.

What Happens After Everything Is Connected

After approval and linking:

- Estimated earnings appear in the **Analytics** section of YouTube Studio**.**
- Finalized earnings and payouts appear in AdSense**.**
- Payments are issued monthly once you hit the payout threshold.

YouTube pays creators consistently, but only after verification, review, and compliance are complete.

A Realistic Reminder

Setting up AdSense does not mean money starts immediately. Most creators spend months building content, trust, and consistency before monetization becomes meaningful. AdSense is infrastructure, not a shortcut. Its value comes once your channel has momentum.

By setting it up now, you're simply removing future obstacles.

Your Action Steps for Today

1. Create your Google AdSense account. Visit **adsense. google.com** and complete the setup carefully.

2. Double-check your information. Make sure your name, address, tax information, and country details are accurate and match official records.

Optional Reflection

What would earning from YouTube represent for you (extra income, creative validation, flexibility, or long-term freedom)? Keep that motivation in mind as you continue building.

You're setting up the system now so it can work for you later.

Tomorrow, we'll walk through how to **make your first video,** so you can start taking practical steps on this journey.

Week 2: Building Your Creator Setup (Simple, Smart, Sustainable)

With your channel in place and your first video planned, it's time to move from preparation to production. Week 2 is about creating a setup that supports you; not one that slows you down or makes starting feel complicated.

In 2026, successful creators don't rely on expensive equipment or studio-level setups. They rely on clarity, consistency, and systems that are easy to repeat. This week will help you build a filming process that fits your space, your budget, and your lifestyle, using tools you likely already have.

You'll learn how to record clean audio, capture flattering light with minimal effort, and set up a filming area that looks intentional without feeling overproduced. You'll also explore editing software and basic tech considerations so your workflow feels smooth instead of overwhelming.

By the end of this week, you won't just understand what you could use; you'll know exactly what works for you. You'll put everything into practice by filming a low-pressure test clip, giving you confidence before you publish anything publicly.

No fancy gear. No complicated setups. Just practical choices that make creating easier, more sustainable, and easier to stick with long-term.

This is where filming stops feeling intimidating and starts feeling doable.

Day 8: Designing Your First Video + A Simple Weekly System

You've spent the past week building the groundwork, setting up your channel, defining your direction, and understanding how YouTube functions. Today is where that preparation turns into something concrete. You're not just thinking about creating anymore. You're planning your first piece of content. This moment matters, not because the video needs to be perfect, but because planning removes hesitation. Once you know what you're making and why, everything else becomes easier.

Why Planning Early Matters

One of the biggest reasons new creators stall is waiting for the **right time**. Better gear. More confidence. A better idea. In 2026, momentum matters more than polish. YouTube fundamentally favors creators who have the courage to publish, learn, and adjust in real-time. It is vital to remember that your first video is not meant to define your channel's legacy forever; its true purpose is to trigger the **feedback loop**. The faster you bridge the gap between having an idea and completing an upload, the faster you will discover the unique rhythm that works for both you and your audience. Instead of viewing your debut as a high-stakes performance, think of it as a **prototype**. It is a necessary first draft that provides you with the data and experience you need to make the next video even better.

What Your First Video Actually Needs to Do

Your first video doesn't need to explain everything about you or your channel. It only needs to do a few things well:

- Be **clear** about what the video is offering.
- Be **simple** enough to create with your current setup.
- Be **relevant** to the niche and audience you've chosen.
- Feel honest and natural in delivery.

YouTube success is driven by viewer experience, especially in the first thirty to sixty seconds of the video. That means clarity beats complexity every time.

Beginner-Friendly First Video Formats (That Still Work Now)

Here are formats that remain effective in 2026 and are low-pressure for new creators:

- A focused introduction video (what this channel will explore).
- A short tutorial or explanation answering a common question in your niche.
- A list-style video ("3 mistakes beginners make when…").
- A reaction or commentary on a current topic in your niche.
- A simple review or walkthrough of something you use.
- A casual vlog with a clear theme or takeaway.

You don't need to cover everything at once. One idea. One purpose. One video.

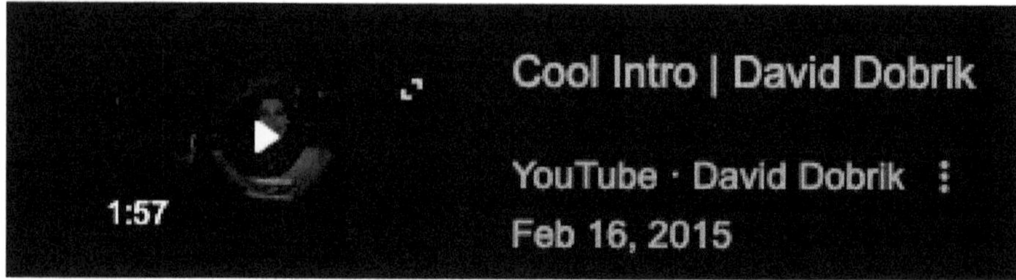

A good real-world example is **David Dobrik's first video**. It was simple, personal, and not overproduced, basically just a short, casual vlog. It didn't try to be perfect or viral. It just showed personality and gave viewers a reason to come back. That's exactly the kind of energy you want for your first upload.

Developing Your Creative Instinct

One of the most overlooked **tools** for a creator isn't a piece of software; it's your **taste**. In 2026, the best creators are also the best students of the platform. Watching YouTube is essential if you want to succeed on it, but you have to watch with **creator eyes**.

Studying strong video formats, thumbnails, and titles builds a creative instinct that eventually becomes second nature. It helps you understand what makes a viewer stop scrolling and start watching.

- **Build a Swipe File:** When you're browsing and a thumbnail makes you stop, don't just click. Pause. Take a screenshot. Ask yourself: Why did that work? Was it the bright colors? The expression? The question it raised in my mind? Save these in a folder for inspiration when you're stuck.
- **Reverse-Engineer Success:** Find a channel you admire and look at their most popular videos. Notice the patterns. Do they always film in the same place? What were their first videos like? You aren't copying them; you are learning the **language** of your niche.
- **Input Controls Output:** If you only watch low-quality content, your brain will think that's the standard. Surround yourself with high-quality creators to elevate your understanding of what a **good** video feels like.

Tip: Watching YouTube isn't procrastination if you do it to study the craft; it's research. Use the **taste** you've developed through research to guide you as you move into the actual planning phase for your first upload.

Plan Your First Video in a Way That Fits

Now that you've started to recognize what makes a video work, let's apply those observations to your own content.

Step 1: Pick a clear topic

Choose something that:

- Helps, explains, or entertains.
- Fits your niche.
- Feels achievable this week.

If someone clicked on your video, what would they hope to get from it?

Step 2: Map the structure (not a full script)

Instead of scripting every word, outline the flow:

- **Opening:** Why should someone keep watching?
- **Core content:** Your main idea, steps, or story.
- **Wrap-up:** One simple takeaway or next step.

This keeps your video focused and easier to film.

Step 3: Decide the format

Ask yourself:

- Am I speaking to the camera?
- Recording my screen?
- Using voice-over with visuals?

Choose the option that feels least complicated. In 2026, authenticity and clarity outperform high production.

Your Weekly Content Checklist (Keep This Handy)

Use this checklist whenever you plan content, not just today:

□ I know who this video is for.

□ I know the main idea of the video.

□ I've outlined the key points.

□ I've chosen a simple format.

□ I've picked a filming day.

□ I'm aiming for progress, not perfection.

This is your repeatable system. Simple systems are what keep creators consistent.

Your Action Steps for Today

1. Choose and outline your first video. Write down the topic and a short outline. Keep it focused and doable.

2. Schedule a filming day. Pick a specific day in the next week and block time for filming. Treat it like an appointment, not a suggestion.

Optional Reflection

What do you want someone to **feel or understand** after watching your video? Write one sentence to guide you while filming.

Tomorrow, we move into **Week 2**, where things get practical. You'll learn what equipment actually matters in 2026, and what you can safely ignore when you're just starting out.

You've built the foundation. Now you're ready to create.

Day 9: What You Actually Need to Start (And What You Don't)

By now, you've done something many people never do: you've committed to starting. As you get closer to filming, it's normal for a new question to surface: *Am I equipped enough to do this properly?* The answer is almost always **yes**. The biggest misconception new creators have is that quality content begins with expensive tools. In reality, most channels stall not because of bad gear, but because creators wait too long to begin. Momentum matters more than equipment, especially at the start.

The Equipment Myth (And Why It Slows People Down)

Scroll through YouTube and you'll see creators with cinematic lighting, studio microphones, and polished backdrops. What's easy to forget is that very few of them started that way. YouTube does not require:

- Professional cameras
- Studio lighting
- High-end microphones
- Paid editing software

What it does reward is:

- Clear visuals
- Understandable audio
- A focused idea
- Consistent effort

If your content is helpful, interesting, or relatable, viewers will stay, even if it's filmed simply.

Your Phone Is More Than Enough

Most modern smartphones can record in high definition or better. When used intentionally, a phone can produce footage that looks clean, sharp, and professional enough for YouTube. Many successful creators started this way. For example, MrBeast has openly talked about filming his early videos with very basic equipment and upgrading only after he understood what worked. The focus was on ideas, not gear. Here are some additional tips that make a big difference:

- Use the rear camera if possible.
- Film horizontally for long-form videos.
- Keep the camera stable (a tripod, shelf, or stack of books works).
- Clean your lens before recording.
- Lock focus and exposure if your phone allows it.

You don't need complexity; you need stability and clarity.

A Note on Faceless Channels

Not every YouTube channel requires you to be on camera. In 2026, **faceless channels are more common than ever**, and many perform extremely well. These channels focus on voice, visuals, or screen-based content rather than a visible presenter.

Examples include:

- Tutorials using screen recordings.
- Commentary with voice-over.
- Educational explainers with visuals or slides.
- Product walkthroughs.
- Animation or text-based storytelling.
- B-roll-driven content (extra footage that plays while you speak).

If being on camera feels too intimidating, that's not a sign of weakness; it's simply a creative choice. YouTube rewards clarity and value, not face time. You can always transition to on-camera content later if you choose.

What Actually Improves Video Quality First

When creators do upgrade, the biggest improvements usually come in this order:

1. **Lighting:** Natural window light or a basic light source.
2. **Audio:** Clear sound matters more than sharp visuals.
3. **Stability:** Keeping the camera still instantly raises quality.

4. **Editing workflow:** Clean cuts and pacing over fancy effects.
5. **Camera upgrades:** Only when your current setup limits you.

Notice that the camera is placed last on the list for a reason: cameras are merely tools to capture your vision, not shortcuts to creating a successful channel. While high-quality equipment can enhance your presentation, it cannot replace the foundational elements of a compelling story, a clear message, and a genuine connection with your audience.

Why Waiting for Better Gear Backfires

It is incredibly tempting to tell yourself, "I'll start my channel as soon as I get that new microphone," or "I just need a better camera before I can film my first lesson." While this feels like being productive, it is often just a **delay disguised as preparation.** The truth is that the most expensive equipment in the world won't make you a better storyteller. In fact, over-complicating your setup early on can actually make it harder to start because you'll spend more time fighting with cables and settings than actually talking to your audience. On YouTube, the fastest way to get better is a very simple cycle:

1. **Film:** Use what you have right now (even if it's just your phone).
2. **Review:** Watch your footage and notice one small thing you can improve.
3. **Adjust:** Fix that one thing in the next video.
4. **Repeat:** Keep the momentum going.

Your first videos aren't meant to be your **magnum opus** or your greatest masterpieces; **they are meant to be your practice field.** They exist to teach you how to stand in front of a lens, to organize your thoughts, and to find your unique rhythm.

By starting with the gear you already own, you remove the barriers to entry and allow yourself to focus on the only thing that truly matters: **connecting with your viewers.** Remember, your audience is there for your knowledge and your personality, not the brand of your camera.

Your Action Steps for Today

1. Take stock of what you already have.

Write down everything you could realistically use to film today. For most beginners, this includes:

- A smartphone or basic camera.
- A quiet space.
- Natural light from a window.
- Built-in mic or wired headphones.

2. Commit to starting without upgrades.

Decide, on paper, that you'll film your first video using what you already own. Future upgrades are allowed. Delays are not.

Optional Reflection

What piece of equipment did you assume you needed before today? How does letting go of that expectation change how soon you can start?

Tomorrow, we'll focus on **making what you already have look and sound better with** practical lighting, framing, and audio tips; no expensive tools are required.

You don't need more gear. You need to begin.

Day 10: Camera Confidence, Audio Clarity, and Viewer Trust

You've made the decision to press record, and that alone puts you ahead of most people who never get past the idea stage. Today is about making sure your video feels comfortable to watch and easy to trust, even if you're filming at home with simple tools. Viewers don't expect perfection, but they **do** expect clarity. If they can see you clearly, hear you clearly, and feel at ease watching you, they'll stay. That's what we're building today.

Camera Confidence Is Built, Not Found

Almost everyone feels awkward talking to a camera at first. That's normal. Confidence on camera doesn't come from waiting until you feel ready; it comes with practice. A few ways to make this easier:

- Talk as if one person is watching, not an audience.
- Keep early recordings short and low-pressure.
- Let your flow feel natural rather than overly scripted.
- Practice with clips you don't plan on publishing.

Your first videos are not a reflection of your potential. They're practice. Every recording makes the next one easier.

Looking Intentional (Not Overproduced)

You don't need a full makeup look, but you do need to look like you showed up on purpose. That means:

- Clean, simple clothing that doesn't distract.
- A tidy background with minimal clutter.
- Relaxed posture and eye contact with the camera.

Viewers subconsciously trust creators who appear prepared, even in casual settings. Effort matters more than polish.

Lighting: The Fastest Visual Upgrade You Can Make

Lighting affects video quality more than most cameras ever will, especially when filming on a phone.

Start with natural light

- Sit facing a window.
- Film during daylight when possible.
- Avoid having bright light behind you.
- Skip harsh overhead lighting.

Budget lighting options (optional)

If you can't rely on natural light, or you just want a simple way to make your videos look clearer and more professional, these affordable ring lights are great starter options:

- **Sensyne 10-inch ring light with tripod**: About **$25–$35**. The **ten-inch (twenty-five cm)** ring light includes a phone holder and multiple brightness modes, making it a solid starter option for YouTube filming or livestreaming.
- **Smaller selfie-style ring lights**: Usually **eight to twelve inches** (twenty to thirty cm) in diameter and often **under $30 USD**.
- **UBeesize 10-inch LED ring light with tripod**: Typically **$30 to $40**. Also **ten inches (twenty-five cm)** across, this light offers adjustable angles and brightness levels, which is helpful if you want more flexibility for different shooting setups.

These work well for desk or tabletop videos when you're filming close to the camera. They are USB-powered and designed for simple setups. They won't replace professional studio kits, but they're an excellent way to get softer, more flattering light on your face without spending a lot.

Using one of these budget options will help your videos look noticeably more polished, especially when you're filming indoors or during darker hours.

A compact ring light:

- Keeps your face evenly lit.
- Reduces shadows and grain.
- Works well for talking-head videos and tutorials.

You don't need maximum brightness, just enough light to keep your face clear and evenly lit.

Audio Matters More Than Video Quality

If viewers can't hear you clearly, they won't stay, no matter how good the video looks. Improve audio with what you already have:

- Record in a quiet room.
- Use soft furnishings (curtains, rugs, pillows) to reduce echo.
- Sit closer to your recording device.
- Test wired headphones with a built-in mic.

Beginner-friendly microphone upgrades

If you want noticeably better sound without spending much, consider:

- **Lavalier (clip-on) microphone**: Usually **$15 to $40.** These clip onto your shirt and work well for talking-to-camera videos. They're simple, portable, and much clearer than most built-in mics.
- **USB condenser microphone**: Usually **$40 to $100.** Best for voiceovers, tutorials, podcasts, and screen recordings. These plug directly into a computer and provide clean, full audio with minimal setup.

A great habit to start right now is the **ten-second rule**. Before you dive into your full recording session, always take a moment to do a short test run. It might feel like an extra step when you are excited to get started, but filming just ten seconds of footage and playing it back can save your entire project. This quick check ensures that your voice is crisp and clear and that your equipment is working exactly as it should, giving you the peace of mind to film your full video with confidence.

Simple Framing Tips That Instantly Improve Your Videos

- Keep the camera at **eye level.**
- Position your eyes about **one-third from the top of the frame.**
- Use a tripod or stable surface (no handheld shots).
- Lock focus and exposure on your phone if possible.
- Make sure nothing distracting appears behind you.

These small choices make your videos feel calm, professional, and easier to watch.

If You Upgrade Cameras Later (Not Required Now)

If you eventually decide your phone isn't enough, many creators choose compact, creator-friendly cameras that offer better autofocus, flip screens, and reliable video quality, without costing as much as a professional rig. Here are a few options you might consider once you're filming consistently:

- **Entry-level 4K compact cameras (~$150 to $300)**: Beginner-oriented cameras with 4K recording and flip screens that help you frame yourself for vlogs and everyday content. These won't match the quality of the more expensive products, but they give you more creative flexibility than a phone alone.
- **Mid-range vlogging cameras with flip screens (~$300 to $600)**: Slightly more capable than basic compacts and still affordable for creators who want smoother autofocus and extra features without a big investment.
- **Sony ZV-1 (~$800 to $1,000)**: A popular compact camera designed for content creators and vloggers, with a flip-out screen, strong autofocus, and built-in mic support. It's a step up from phone video, especially for talking-to-camera-style videos and high-quality clips.

These kinds of cameras often offer better stabilization, clearer video in varied lighting, and more control over settings, but only if you're already comfortable filming and editing regularly. Until then, your smartphone remains a perfectly valid and powerful starting tool.

The key rule: **upgrade only when your current setup begins to limit your creativity or workflow.** Otherwise you're paying for gear before you're ready to use it.

Your Action Steps for Today

1. Set up your filming space. Use natural light or a small light. Adjust your camera height. Clear your background.

2. Test your audio. Record short clips using two or three options and choose the clearest sound.

3. Practice being on camera. Record a one-minute introduction just for yourself. Watch it back without judgment. Notice one thing you'd improve next time.

Optional Reflection

What helps you feel calm before recording (music, breathing, stretching, silence)? Write down a short pre-filming ritual you can repeat each time.

Tomorrow, we'll move into **editing**: how to turn raw footage into a finished video using simple, beginner-friendly tools.

You don't need perfect gear. You need clarity, consistency, and the courage to press record again.

Day 11: Editing Tools and Software for New Creators

So, you've recorded your first test clip, or maybe you've even filmed a full video. Either way, the next step is the same: **editing**. For many new creators, this is the stage where things suddenly feel complicated. Timelines, buttons, exports, and formats; it's easy to assume you need advanced skills or expensive software to move forward. You don't. At this stage, editing is not about perfection. It's about learning how to **clean up what you filmed**, keep it watchable, and get it ready to upload. That's all.

What Editing Really Means Right Now

When you're just starting out, editing is simply the process of:

- Cutting out mistakes, long pauses, or repeated takes.
- Making sure clips are in the right order.
- Adjusting audio so your voice is clear.
- Adding light text or captions if they help understanding.
- Exporting the video in good quality.

You are not expected to add complex effects, animations, or cinematic transitions. In fact, doing less usually leads to better videos early on. Clear, simple, and easy-to-follow beats flashy every time.

Choosing Software Without Overcomplicating It

Before downloading anything, ground your choice in a few practical questions:

- Am I editing on my **phone** or on a **computer**?
- Do I want something that feels very simple, or something I can grow into?
- Am I okay with a free version for now?
- Am I mostly making long videos, Shorts, or a mix of both?

There is no single **best** editor. There is only the editor that fits your current setup and comfort level.

Editing on Your Phone or Tablet

If you're filming on your phone, today's mobile editing apps are powerful enough to handle real YouTube videos, especially Shorts and other short-form content.

1. CapCut. One of the most popular mobile editors for creators right now. It's fast, intuitive, and built for speed. You can trim clips, add captions, drop in music, and export quickly without needing technical knowledge. It's especially useful if you plan to post Shorts regularly or want quick edits without sitting at a computer.

2. InShot. Offers a straightforward timeline-style editor that feels very beginner-friendly. It's great for simple cuts, text overlays, and basic transitions. If you want something clean and predictable, this is a solid choice.

3. VN Video Editor. A powerful but underrated mobile editor. It gives you more control than most phone apps while staying free and watermark-free. It's a good option if you want to grow your editing skills on mobile without jumping to a laptop yet.

Editing on a Laptop or PC

If you're editing on a computer, you'll generally have more control, better file management, and more flexibility, especially for longer videos.

1. Movavi Video Editor: Movavi is designed with beginners in mind. The interface is clean, drag-and-drop, and easy to understand on day one. You can trim clips, add titles, transitions, and music without feeling overwhelmed. Recent versions also include smart features like auto subtitles, noise removal, silence detection, and background removal. These tools help speed up editing and reduce frustration, especially when you're still learning.

2. iMovie (Mac): If you're on a Mac, iMovie is already available and more than enough for your first videos. It's simple, stable, and intentionally limited so you don't get lost in settings. For basic YouTube videos (vlogs, reviews, and talking-head content), iMovie does the job well.

3. DaVinci Resolve: DaVinci Resolve is a powerful, professional-grade editor that's available for free. It combines editing, color grading, audio, and effects in one program. That power comes with complexity. It's not the easiest place to start, but it's an excellent option if you're serious about learning editing long-term and want cinematic control later on.

4. Adobe Premiere Pro: Premiere Pro remains a strong choice for creators who want maximum flexibility and deep control. It integrates with other Adobe tools and supports complex workflows. However, it comes with a high monthly cost and can be demanding on older computers, making it better suited for creators who already know they'll commit to long-term production.

5. Shotcut: Shotcut is a free, open-source editor that works on Windows, macOS, and Linux. It doesn't look as polished as paid software, but it offers solid editing tools with no watermark or subscription. If you want full control without paying for software, Shotcut is a reliable option once you get used to the interface.

Simple Editing Guidelines for Beginners

- **Place your clips in a clear order.** If you recorded multiple clips, line them up in the order you want them to appear. Don't worry about transitions yet; clean cuts are perfectly fine.

- **Start by cutting mistakes and long pauses.** Remove obvious errors, repeated takes, long silences, or moments where you're setting up or thinking. If something doesn't add value to the video, it can usually go.

- **Keep text minimal and easy to read.** Use text only when it adds clarity, such as highlighting a key point or labeling a section. Short phrases work best. Avoid filling the screen with too many words.

- **Make sure your voice is always clear.** Your voice should be the loudest and most important sound. If you use music, make sure it's copyright-free (more on this on *Day 21: Copyright, Fair Use, and Monetization Safety*) and keep it low so it supports the video instead of competing with it.

- **Don't overuse effects or transitions.** Simple cuts look more professional than flashy effects. If a transition draws attention to itself, it's probably unnecessary.

- **Stop editing when the video makes sense.** Once your video flows, sounds clear, and gets your point across, it's done. Extra polishing rarely matters at this stage.

• **Export in 1080p or higher.** This ensures your video looks crisp on YouTube across phones, tablets, and computers. Even simple videos benefit from good export quality.

• **Remember what this stage is for.** Your first videos are about learning how editing works, not impressing. Every upload makes the next one easier.

Your Action Steps for Today

1. **Decide where you'll edit.** Choose whether you'll edit on your phone or on a computer. Don't overthink it; pick the option that feels easiest to start with.

2. **Choose one editing tool.** Select a single editing app or software and commit to it for now. Sticking with one tool helps you learn faster and avoid confusion.

3. **Import a test clip.** Open the editor and bring in a short clip you've already recorded. This is just for practice, not for publishing.

4. **Practice the basics.** Trim the beginning and end, adjust the audio so your voice is clear, and try a simple export. Focus on becoming familiar with the workflow, not perfection.

5. **Save and review your file.** Save the finished video and watch it back once. The goal is familiarity and confidence, not flawless editing.

6. **Use learning resources intentionally.** Once you've chosen your editor, look up one or two beginner tutorials on YouTube or skim the software's official guide. Learn only what you need right now; avoid falling into the watch-everything trap.

Optional Reflection

Which part of editing felt more difficult than you expected? Which part felt easier? Write it down; you'll notice how quickly your confidence builds over the next few videos.

Tomorrow, we'll look at **AI-powered editing tools built directly into YouTube** and how you can use them to speed up production.

Day 12: Using AI Editing Tools Inside YouTube

Until recently, editing meant leaving YouTube, opening another app, exporting a file, and uploading it again. In 2026, that workflow has changed. YouTube now includes **built-in AI editing tools** designed to help creators, especially beginners, turn raw footage into usable videos directly inside the platform. These tools don't replace editing software, but they **reduce friction**, speed things up, and make starting much easier.

What YouTube's AI Editing Tools Are Meant to Do

YouTube's AI editing features are designed to:

- Help you create a **first draft** faster.
- Simplify cutting, pacing, and structuring.
- Reduce the technical editing skills needed at the start.
- Make Shorts editing quicker and more playful.

They are **assistive**, not automatic publishing tools. You are still in control of what gets uploaded.

Edit with AI (For Shorts)

If you've ever felt overwhelmed by a gallery full of video clips and weren't sure how to piece them together, you are going to love **Edit with AI**. This is currently YouTube's most beginner-friendly editing feature, designed to take the **heavy lifting** out of creating Shorts. Instead of spending hours trimming and syncing, you can let YouTube's intelligent system act as your personal assistant editor, turning your raw moments into a polished story in seconds.

What It Does

When you upload raw clips for Shorts, **Edit with AI** can:

- Analyze your footage.
- Cut it into a coherent short video.

- Apply basic pacing and style.
- Add music that matches the tone.

Think of it as an **auto-assembled rough cut**.

How to Use It

1. Open the Shorts creation flow in YouTube.
2. Upload one or more raw clips.
3. Choose **Edit with AI.**
4. Let YouTube generate a draft.
5. Manually tweak cuts, music, or timing before posting.

Use this when:

- You feel stuck staring at raw clips.
- You want a fast starting point.
- You're experimenting with Shorts formats.

AI Backgrounds, Motion, and Visual Edits (Shorts)

Sometimes, the biggest challenge in making a video isn't the script or the lighting; it's the environment around you. We've all been there: you have a great idea, but your room is messy, your background is a plain white wall, or the shot just feels a bit **flat**. In 2026, YouTube has introduced a suite of **AI-powered visual tools** specifically for Shorts that allow you to transform your space and add professional flair without needing a Hollywood budget or a green screen. These tools are like having a digital set designer and a special effects team right inside your phone. They allow you to manipulate the **world** of your video with just a few taps, making your content more immersive and visually exciting.

What These Tools Do

You can:

- Replace or generate backgrounds (with sound).
- Add motion to static shots.

- Restyle the look of a clip.
- Add simple visual props or effects.

These features are especially useful if:

- Your background is plain or distracting.
- You don't have space for a filming setup.
- You want more visual interest without complex editing.

How to Use Them

1. Start editing a Short.
2. Select the background or visual tools.
3. Choose a generated background or motion style.
4. Preview the result.
5. Adjust or remove anything that feels distracting.

Try not to overload your video with too many visual changes. A single, well-placed shift in visuals is usually all you need to hold attention and keep things engaging.

Speech-to-Song (Creative Editing Tool)

If you have ever recorded a line of dialogue that was particularly funny, rhythmic, or memorable, you might want to try one of YouTube's most playful new features: **Speech-to-Song**. This tool is powered by advanced music models, and it allows you to remix the spoken words in your video into a catchy, musical soundtrack for your Shorts.

What It Does

- Converts speech into a song-like soundtrack.
- Syncs audio rhythm with the video.

This is not meant for serious or informational videos, but it works well for:

- Humor
- Trend-based Shorts
- Experimental or creative content

How to Use It

1. Upload or record a Short with spoken audio.
2. Select the **Speech-to-Song** option.
3. Preview the generated result.
4. Decide if it fits your content style.

If it doesn't fit, skip it. Not every tool is for every creator.

Auto-Captions and Audio Cleanup

Inside YouTube, AI can also help with basic but essential editing tasks. Even the most visually stunning video can be hard to watch if the audio is messy or if the viewer can't follow along in a noisy environment. Captions are no longer just an **extra** feature; they are a vital part of how people consume video today, especially on mobile, where many viewers watch with the sound turned off. While you can find your caption settings under the **Subtitles** (or sometimes the updated **Languages**) tab in the left-hand menu, the AI does most of the heavy lifting during the upload process.

Auto-Captions

- Automatically generates captions for your video.
- Improves accessibility and retention.
- Especially useful for Shorts and mobile viewers.

How to use: Enable captions during upload or inside YouTube Studio, then review and correct errors. (These are detailed in Day 19: *Descriptions, Keywords, and Signals That Matter in 2026*).

Audio Enhancement

Nothing turns a viewer away faster than a **hissing** background hum or a voice that is muffled and hard to hear. YouTube has now made professional-grade audio accessible to everyone by integrating **AI Audio Cleanup** directly into the Shorts editor and the **YouTube Create** app. This tool is designed to act like a professional sound engineer, isolating your voice and removing the **noise** of the real world. During editing, simply enable audio enhancement options and preview the result. Always listen back before publishing.

How Beginners Should Use AI Editing Tools

As you start experimenting with these new features, it is helpful to follow one simple, golden rule: Let the AI start the edit, but you must be the one to finish it. Think of AI as your **intern**; it is excellent at doing the tedious, time-consuming work, but it lacks your unique perspective, your humor, and your heart.

The most effective way to use these tools is to let them handle the **blank canvas** phase. If you have thirty minutes of raw footage and you feel overwhelmed, let an AI tool like **Edit with AI** create that first draft. This gives you a foundation to build upon. AI is also incredibly helpful for tasks that used to take hours of manual labor, such as:

- Cutting down raw footage to find the most interesting moments.
- Generating captions so your content is immediately accessible to everyone.
- Cleaning up audio so you can film anywhere without worrying about a perfect studio setup.

While these tools are impressive, there are a few traps to avoid as you grow your channel. The biggest risk is letting the technology override your own personality. If an AI generates a music track or a background that feels off or doesn't match your message, don't be afraid to change it. Your audience is subscribing to **you**, not a set of algorithms.

To maintain that professional quality, avoid the temptation to use every AI effect at once. Too many **generated backgrounds** or **Speech-to-Song** filters can make your video feel cluttered and distracting. Finally, never hit **Publish** without a full human review. AI can occasionally misinterpret a word in your captions or cut a clip a second too early, and those tiny errors can break the immersion for your viewer.

At the end of the day, remember that your personality matters more than perfect polish. Use AI to remove the friction of editing, but keep your hands on the steering wheel to ensure the final video feels authentically yours.

Your Action Steps for Today

1. Open YouTube's editing tools. Go to YouTube Shorts or YouTube Studio and enter the editing or creation flow. You don't need a finished video; this is just for exploration.

2. Upload a raw clip. Choose a short, unedited clip you've already recorded. This can be messy or imperfect; it's only for testing.

3. Generate a first draft with AI. Use **Edit with AI** to automatically create a rough version of your video. Let the tool do the initial cutting and pacing.

4. Test one additional AI editing feature. Pick **one** feature to try, such as auto-captions, background changes, or motion effects. Keep it simple and focused.

5. Review and adjust manually. Watch the edited video and make small changes where needed. You're looking for clarity, not polish.

6. Decide what's worth keeping. Notice which AI tools actually helped you and ignore the rest. One or two useful features are more than enough

Optional Reflection

Which AI editing feature saved you the most time? Which one felt unnecessary or distracting?

Tomorrow, we'll focus on **workflow and consistency**, which involves combining filming, editing, AI tools, and publishing into a routine that's sustainable long-term.

Day 13: Creating a Repeatable Filming Setup

By now, you've started filming, explored editing tools, and tested your workflow. The next step is making sure everything around that process, **your filming space and your computer setup**, can support you consistently. This chapter brings two things together:

- A **repeatable filming setup** you can return to anytime.
- A **reliable tech setup** (laptop + internet) that won't slow you down.

You don't need the newest laptop, the fastest Wi-Fi plan, or a home studio. All you need is a setup that works reliably and doesn't create friction every time you want to film or upload.

What Repeatable Really Means

A repeatable setup is one you can rely on every time you record. It should look mostly the same each session, take just a few minutes to put together rather than hours of tweaking, and work well without needing perfect lighting, sound, or conditions. Most importantly, it should free up your mental energy so you can focus on speaking naturally and delivering your content, instead of constantly troubleshooting equipment or adjusting your environment. Professional doesn't mean expensive. It means **intentional, stable, and easy to recreate**.

Choosing Your Filming Spot

Start with one place you can realistically use again and again. Look for a spot that is:

- Quiet enough to record.
- Easy to light consistently.
- Comfortable to sit or stand in.
- Simple to reset if something moves.

This could be a corner of your room, a desk, a kitchen table, or any small area that stays relatively unchanged. The goal isn't perfection; it's **consistency**.

Setting Up the Frame

Background

Your background should support your video, not compete with it.

Keep it:

- Clean and uncluttered.
- Visually calm.
- Loosely connected to your content.

Quick fixes:

- Remove laundry, cables, and random items.
- Close doors or closets if possible.
- Keep décor minimal and intentional.

If the background doesn't distract, it's doing its job.

Camera Position

Camera placement affects how professional your video feels.

- Place the camera at **eye level or slightly above.**
- Avoid filming from below or extreme angles.
- Frame yourself with head-and-shoulders visible and some space above your head.

Once you find a good angle, **stick with it**. Use books, boxes, or a tripod to recreate the same height each time.

Lighting

Consistency in the way you light up your videos matters more than complex lighting systems.

- Light should come from **in front of you.**
- Avoid strong backlighting from windows behind you.
- Use the same light source each time if possible.

If you rely on daylight, film around the same time of day. If you use a lamp or ring light, keep it in the same position every time.

Your Computer Setup (The Often-Ignored Part)

A repeatable filming setup only works if your computer can handle editing and uploads without constant issues. You do **not** need a high-end device, but you do need a reliable one.

What to Look For in a Laptop or Desktop

If you're using (or buying) a computer, aim for:

- **Relatively recent hardware:** From the last three to five years.
- **At least 8 GB of RAM:** Helps prevent freezing and lag during editing.
- **Enough storage:** 256 GB is the bare minimum; external storage helps.
- Examples of external storage include:
    - Portable external hard drives (1–2 TB) for storing raw footage and finished videos.
    - External SSDs for faster access and quicker file transfers.
    - USB flash drives for temporary transfers or backups (not ideal for long-term storage).
- **A decent processor:** Something comparable to an Intel i5 or Apple M1 (faster processors mean smoother editing and quicker exports).
- **Good battery life (for laptops):** Especially helpful if you edit or upload while traveling or working outside your main filming space.

If your computer regularly crashes, lags badly, or runs out of space, it will slow down your entire creative process, even if everything else is working well. If you're unsure about your system, check your device settings or ask for advice at a computer shop. If you're shopping, simply say you need a device for **light video editing and content creation**; that's enough context. Even if you film and edit on your phone, a computer is still useful for:

- Uploading videos.
- Designing thumbnails.
- Managing YouTube Studio and your channel.

Internet Speed Matters More Than You Think

Uploading your content is often the stage where the excitement of creating hits the reality of technical hurdles. It is common for creators to find themselves stuck at this final hurdle; a slow or unstable internet connection can easily turn what should be a five-minute upload into an hour-long exercise in frustration.

Recommended Upload Speeds

- **At least Five Mbps** for HD videos.
- **10+ Mbps** is ideal for regular uploads or livestreams.

You can check your speed using a basic online speed test like speedtest.net. If your upload speed is slow:

- Use a **wired Ethernet connection** if possible.
- Upload during off-peak hours.
- Export slightly smaller file sizes without sacrificing quality.

A reliable connection makes consistency much easier.

Keep Everything Consistent

The real goal is reducing decision fatigue. Try to:

- Film in the same spot whenever possible.
- Use the same camera angle and lighting setup.
- Keep your filming gear together.
- Use the same computer and upload routine.

When your setup becomes familiar, filming stops feeling like a task you need to prepare for.

Common Mistakes to Avoid

- Changing your filming location every video.
- Messy or distracting backgrounds.
- Light behind you instead of in front.
- Camera angles that feel awkward or unflattering.
- Ignoring storage or internet limitations.

These don't make you more creative; they just add friction.

Your Action Steps for Today

1. Choose your default filming spot. Pick one place you can realistically return to most of the time.

2. Set and test your frame. Position your camera, check your background, and record a short test clip.

3. Confirm your computer is ready. Check available storage, close unnecessary apps, and make sure your editing software runs smoothly.

4. Test your internet upload speed. Notice whether uploads feel manageable or frustrating.

5. Create a simple setup checklist. Write down your filming spot, camera position, lighting source, and computer setup so you can repeat it easily.

Optional Reflection

Does your current setup make filming feel easier or harder? What's one small change, physical or technical, that would remove friction next time?

Tomorrow, you'll put everything together for a **full test run**: filming a complete video using your chosen setup, tools, and workflow.

Consistency isn't about motivation. It's about making starting feel effortless.

Day 14: Practice Day: Filming Without Pressure or Perfection

You've spent the last two weeks setting things up (your gear, your space, your software, and your workflow). Today isn't about launching or impressing anyone. Today is about **practice**. This is your first real filming day, but with one important rule: **nothing you record today needs to be published.** The ultimate goal for your first few uploads is to prioritize personal comfort over production quality and to build genuine confidence rather than chasing professional polish. By focusing on how you feel behind the camera rather than how the video looks to a critic, you lower the stakes and make it much easier to show up consistently. Every creator you admire started exactly here, talking to a camera, feeling awkward, overthinking their voice, and noticing every "um." That phase isn't a failure; it's the entry point.

Why This Practice Matters

Filming without pressure lets you:

- Get used to seeing yourself on camera.
- Learn how your voice sounds when recorded.
- Test your setup in real conditions.
- Build confidence speaking without stopping.
- Discover what feels natural for **you**.

You're not training for a viral moment. You're training your nervous system to treat the camera like a normal thing.

What You're Practicing Today

This is a private test run to explore:

- Your camera angle and framing.
- Lighting placement.
- Audio clarity.
- How you speak on camera.
- How it feels to watch yourself back.
- (Optionally) basic editing with your own footage.

Even one minute of footage counts. The value is in **doing**, not in duration.

What to Say in Your Test Clip

Keep it simple and familiar. You're not performing; you're talking. Choose **one** of the following:

- A short **"about me"** introduction.
- A rough version of your first video idea.
- Why you decided to start this channel.
- An answer to a common question in your niche.
- A casual draft of a channel trailer, which tells new viewers who you are, what your channel is about, and why they should stick around. Think of it as your channel's welcome message.

Write a few bullet points if it helps, but don't script every word. You want to hear how you **actually** speak.

While You're Filming

A few gentle guidelines:

- Keep it short: **one to three minutes is enough.**
- Use your full setup (camera, light, mic, and background).
- Record more than one take if you want.
- Talk like you would to a friend, not an audience.
- Don't try to sound like other creators.
- Smile a little more than feels natural; it reads well on camera.

If you mess up, pause and continue. You don't need to restart every time.

Watching It Back (This Part Matters)

When you review the footage:

- Don't judge your appearance or voice.
- Don't compare yourself to anyone online.
- Look for **one thing you liked.**

- Note **one thing to improve next time.**

That's the secret to long-term growth: focusing on one win and one adjustment at a time ensures you're moving forward without being overwhelmed. By treating this process as constructive feedback rather than harsh criticism, you give yourself the mental space to improve without the weight of perfectionism.

Optional: Light Editing Practice

If you want to go one step further, import the clip into your editing software and practice trimming the beginning and end, adjusting the audio levels so everything sounds clear and balanced, adding a simple title or name tag, and exporting and saving the file. The goal isn't to polish a perfect final video, but to get comfortable with the process itself, learning each step with zero pressure so it feels easy and natural when it really counts.

Your Action Steps for Today

1. Film a test clip. Use your current setup and talk about something easy. Keep it relaxed and short.

2. Watch it back without judgment. Notice one thing that worked and one thing to adjust next time.

3. Optionally edit the clip. Do a basic trim and export just to get comfortable with the workflow.

Optional Reflection

How did it feel to be on camera for real? What felt natural? What felt awkward but workable? Write a few notes and save them. In a month, you'll be shocked by the difference.

Tomorrow, you begin **Week 3: Turning Ideas Into Published Videos**, where the focus shifts from preparation to actually creating and publishing content. You've practiced enough. Now you're ready to move forward, one video at a time.

Week 3: Turning Ideas Into Published Videos

Your foundation is in place. You've set up your channel, organized your gear, tested your space, and practiced being on camera. Now it's time to move from preparation to **real creation**.

This is the week when your YouTube journey truly starts, not by planning more, but by **making videos people can actually watch**.

Over the next few days, you'll learn how to turn simple ideas into complete YouTube videos. We'll cover how to shape an idea, structure a video, film with intention, edit without overthinking, and upload with confidence. You'll also learn how to hook viewers early, keep them watching, and present your content in a way that feels natural (not forced or overproduced).

Perfection is not the goal this week. Momentum is.

Every video you make will teach you something about your voice, your pacing, your audience, and your process. Some things will work, some won't, and that's exactly how creators grow.

This week is about **showing up, experimenting, and finishing videos**. Each upload is a step toward clarity, confidence, and consistency.

You're no longer preparing to be a creator.

You're becoming one.

Day 15: Planning Your First Content Ecosystem

You're officially moving from preparation into creation. This is where your ideas stop living in your head or your notes app and start becoming real videos on your channel. Before you hit record again, you just need a clear and simple plan for your **first few uploads** and how they connect to each other. It doesn't have to be a complicated content calendar or a long roadmap. The goal today is to build your first content ecosystem, made up of a few long-form videos supported by Shorts that introduce your channel, attract the right viewers, and help you learn and improve quickly as you go. **Why Plan More Than One Video?** One video is a great start, but planning at least three videos creates the momentum needed to move from a **one-off uploader** to a consistent creator.

Planning your first three long-form videos helps you:

- Avoid the "what should I film next?" panic.
- Learn faster by repeating the process.
- Show viewers (and the algorithm) that your channel is active.
- Create connected content instead of random uploads.

These videos don't need to be perfect. They just need to be **finished**.

Thinking in Ecosystems (Not Isolated Videos)

In 2026, YouTube strongly connects **long-form videos and Shorts**. Instead of treating them separately, think of them as working together.

A simple way to start:

- **Long-form videos** are your **deep dives**. This is where you provide the most value, build the deepest trust, and establish your authority.
- **Shorts** are your **digital flyers**. They are designed to grab attention, offer quick highlights, and invite new people into your world.

One long video can easily create:

- Two to five Shorts.
- Multiple entry points for new viewers.
- More chances to be discovered.

You're not just planning **videos**. You're planning **connected content**.

Content that stands out is more likely to be shared. When viewers feel surprised, impressed, or genuinely entertained, they don't just watch; they pass the video along. That sharing effect expands your reach, introduces your channel to new people, and helps you build a more invested audience over time. Creators like **MrBeast** and **Ryan Trahan** are especially strong examples of this approach. Their videos are designed to be clear, intentional, and easy to explain to someone else in a sentence or two. Even if your niche is completely different, studying how top creators structure ideas, frame challenges, or highlight a clear takeaway can teach you a lot about what makes content spread.

You're not meant to copy these creators. Instead, use them as reference points. Pay attention to how their videos communicate purpose quickly, how each idea feels complete, and why someone might think, "I need to send this to someone."

Choosing Your First Three Long-Form Videos

Start with topics that are:

- Easy for **you** to talk about.
- Aligned with your niche or interest.
- Useful, interesting, or relatable to your ideal viewer.
- Realistic to film and edit with your current setup.

Ask yourself: Can I finish this video this week?

Here are some beginner-friendly video types that work in almost any niche:

- **Channel introduction / why this channel exists.**
- **Simple guide or tutorial** (three to six minutes).
- **Personal story, recommendation, or explanation** related to your theme.

These videos introduce:

- Who you are.
- What your channel is about.
- Why someone should keep watching.

Planning Shorts Alongside Long Videos

Once you've chosen your three long videos, move on to the Shorts.

For each long video, think:

- What's one strong moment or takeaway?
- What question does this video answer?
- What sentence would stop someone from scrolling?

Examples of Shorts ideas:

- A bold statement from the video.
- A quick tip pulled from the main content.
- A question you answer in the long video.
- A relatable or funny moment.

You don't need to script Shorts yet; just **note the moments** while planning.

Outline Before You Film

You don't need a full script, but you do need structure.

A simple outline works best:

- **Hook (first five to ten seconds):** Why should someone care?
- **Short intro:** Who you are + what the video is about.
- **Main content:** two to four clear points.
- **Ending / CTA (Call to Action):** Invite viewers to watch another video, comment, or subscribe.

Bullet points are often all you need. They help you stay focused, prevent rambling, and make both filming and editing your video much easier.

Using the YouTube Inspiration Tab (AI-Assisted Planning)

YouTube Studio includes an **Inspiration tab** designed to help creators brainstorm ideas, titles, thumbnails, hooks, and outlines with AI support.

Important Things to Know First

- Ideas are **AI-generated** and may vary in quality.
- Suggestions do **not** represent YouTube's views.
- Don't include personal or sensitive information.
- Use ideas as starting points, not final answers.

The Inspiration tab:

- It is available on **desktop only.**
- Works in **English only.**
- May show more **general suggestions** if you haven't uploaded videos yet.

This doesn't mean that you can't use it if you haven't published any videos. Early ideas may be broader, but they're still useful for brainstorming.

How to Use the Inspiration Tab: Your Step-by-Step Guide

1. **Sign in to YouTube Studio:** Your **backstage** area where you manage every detail of your channel.
2. **Navigate to Content:** Look at the menu on the left side of your screen and click on the **Content** tab. This lists all the videos that you have uploaded.
3. **Find the Inspiration Tab:** Look at the very top of your screen, above your list of videos. You will see several options; click on the one labeled **Inspiration**. This is where the magic happens!
4. **Browse Your Personal Feed:** Once you're in the Inspiration tab, YouTube will show you a handful of ideas specifically picked for your channel based on what your current viewers (and people like them) are watching.
5. **Refine Your Search:** If you have a specific topic in mind, you can use the search box to type in a phrase. You can also click on **suggestion chips**, to help narrow down your ideas.
6. **Dig Deeper:** If an idea catches your eye, click on **More like this**. This tells the tool you are on the right track and asks it to show you similar topics that might be even better.
7. **Build Your Idea Bank:** When you find a spark you love, click the **bookmark icon** (the little flag). This saves the idea into a **Saved** list so you can come back to it whenever you are ready to start filming.

You can also:

- Generate **hooks** for openings.
- Get **outline suggestions** for videos.
- Explore **title ideas** based on trends.
- Preview **thumbnail concepts** (digital painting or sketch styles).
- Check **audience interest indicators** and related videos to see whether people already care about the topic you want to create. You are essentially checking whether viewers are actively searching for it or watching similar content right now.

Use this tool to **spark thinking**, not to outsource judgment.

Best Practices for Using Inspiration (Without Getting Overwhelmed)

- Bring your own ideas first, then refine them with AI.
- Trust your instincts (even low-interest ideas can work with the right angle).
- Look for overlap between what you want to make and what people are curious about.
- Save ideas, then step away and decide later.

Remember, you're still the creative decision-maker.

Your Action Steps for Today

1. Choose your first three long-form video topics. Keep them simple, doable, and aligned with your channel's direction.

2. Brainstorm on how Shorts will support them. For each long video, note one to three moments that could become Shorts.

3. Write a short outline for each video. Use the hook–intro–main content–ending structure. Stick with bullet points only; avoid long, scripted texts.

4. Explore the Inspiration tab (optional but helpful). Use it to refine ideas, hooks, or titles, but don't overuse it. You're not building a content empire today. You're building a starting point.

Optional Reflection

Do these first three videos represent the kind of channel you want to grow into? Do they feel achievable this week, not someday?

Tomorrow, we'll focus on one of the most important skills on YouTube in 2026: **crafting strong hooks that earn the first five seconds of attention**.

Day 16: Hooks That Earn Attention (Not Clickbait)

You can have a great idea, solid filming, and clean editing, but if the opening doesn't land, most viewers won't stay. That's not a reflection of your value or your content; it's simply how YouTube works. People scroll quickly, sample aggressively, and decide in seconds whether a video is worth their time. The platform notices this behavior too, which is why the beginning of your video carries so much weight. Today is about learning how to **earn attention honestly**, without exaggeration or tricks.

What a Hook Really Is

In the fast-paced world of YouTube, your **Hook** is arguably the most important part of your entire video. It is the opening moment, usually within the first minute, where you address the one silent question every viewer is asking as they click: "Why should I keep watching?"

If you don't answer that question immediately, most people will click away before you even finish your introduction. However, a great hook isn't about being loud or **clickbaity**; it is about being a helpful guide. A truly effective hook achieves three specific goals:

- **It Makes the Topic Crystal Clear:** Within the first few seconds, the viewer should know exactly what the video is about. There should be no mystery about whether they are in the right place.
- **It Signals Immediate Value:** You are telling the viewer how their life will improve after watching your video. Will they be entertained? Will they learn a new skill? Will they finally understand a complex topic?
- **It Sets the Roadmap:** You are giving them a **sneak peek** of what is coming up, which builds anticipation and encourages them to stick around until the end.

Many new creators feel pressured to start their videos with high-energy music or shouting at the camera because they think that is what a **hook** looks like. In reality, clarity is more powerful than hype. You don't need fancy graphics or a dramatic performance; you simply need to tell the viewer exactly what you are going to show them and why it matters to them.

A strong hook helps:

- Improve early watch time.
- Increase viewer retention.
- Help new viewers understand your channel faster.
- Make your videos feel confident and intentional.

Without a hook, viewers often leave before your content even begins.

Hooks for Long-Form Videos

For long-form content, hooks should feel **grounded and honest**. You're inviting someone into a conversation, not yelling for attention.

Here are simple hook styles that work consistently:

- **Relatable question:** "Have you ever spent hours on a video only for no one to watch it?"
- **Clear outcome or benefit:** "By the end of this video, you'll know exactly how to plan your first three YouTube uploads."
- **Specific promise:** "Today I'm sharing the three mistakes that slowed my channel down in the first month."
- **Short personal context:** "When I uploaded my first video, I almost quit; here's what I wish I knew instead."

After the hook, briefly introduce yourself and confirm what the video will cover. Keep this transition short and natural; no long intros.

Hooks for Shorts (Different, Faster Rules)

In the world of Shorts, you don't have time to **ease in**. You must start directly inside the action or the main point, **cutting out the fluff** and introductions to grab attention the very second the video begins.

Good Shorts hooks often:

- Begin mid-sentence or mid-action.
- Use bold statements.
- Ask direct questions.
- Show the result first, explanation later.

Examples:

- "Stop doing this if your videos aren't getting views."
- "Nobody tells beginners this about YouTube."
- "I wish someone had told me this before my first upload."

For Shorts, **your hook is the video.** There's no warm-up.

What Makes a Hook Feel Like Clickbait (and How to Avoid It)

Clickbait happens when:

- The promise doesn't match the content.
- The title or opening exaggerates results.
- The video takes too long to deliver value.

To avoid this:

- Be specific, not dramatic.
- Match your hook to your actual content.
- Deliver on what you promise early.

Sometimes, it is easy to get caught up in the idea of **going viral** or creating massive **hype** around a single video. However, it is important to remember that as you start your journey, **trust builds much faster than hype**. While a flashy title might get someone to click once, it is your honesty and consistency that will make them subscribe and come back next week.

Simple Tips That Improve Hooks Immediately

- Practice your hook **out loud** before filming.
- Record the hook multiple times and choose the best take.
- Trim pauses aggressively in the first fifteen seconds.
- Add light energy, slightly more than a normal conversation.
- Let viewers know what's coming next.

One of the best secrets for creating a great opening is to wait until the very end to film it. By waiting until the main content is recorded, you will know exactly what value you are delivering to your audience, which makes it much easier to introduce the topic with genuine energy. This also allows you to look back at your footage and identify which specific part of the video would work as the most effective hook. Sometimes a surprising moment or a key realization happens naturally in the middle of your filming, and highlighting that right at the start is a fantastic way to keep people watching.

Using YouTube's Inspiration Tools to Improve Hooks

To find this feature, start by opening your **YouTube Studio** dashboard. Look at the menu on the left side of your screen and click on **Analytics**. From there, you will see several tabs across the top of the page; click on the one labeled **Research**. Inside that section, you will find the **Inspiration** tool waiting for you.

Once you have opened the **Inspiration** tab, it can act as a wonderful brainstorming partner to help you:

- **Explore hook ideas:** You can see what topics are currently trending and get ideas for how to grab your viewers' attention right away.
- **Analyze successful openings:** It allows you to see how other creators in your niche start their videos, which is a great way to learn what works.
- **Generate fresh angles:** If you are feeling stuck, the tool can help you come up with unique opening lines or different perspectives that you can adapt into your own voice.

Use it as a brainstorming partner, not a scriptwriter. The best hooks should still sound like **you**. Even if you haven't uploaded yet, this inspiration tool can offer **general hook styles and topic angles** to help you brainstorm.

Confirming the Click and Opening Loops

In the world of YouTube, the **Back Button** is your biggest competitor. Viewers decide within the first few seconds if they are going to stay or leave. Great creators don't just start talking; they **confirm the click** and **open new loops.**

1. Confirm the Click Quickly

The moment someone clicks, their brain is asking, "Am I in the right place?" If your title was "How to Fix a Leaky Sink," but you spend the first two minutes talking about your morning coffee, the viewer feels misled. This is where all we learned about hooks comes in handy.

- **The Strategy:** Validate the topic immediately. Within the first five seconds, use a visual or a sentence that mirrors the title.
- **Example:** "If your sink looks like this [point to leak], we're going to fix it in under five minutes without calling a plumber."

2. Open New Loops

Once you've confirmed they are in the right place, you need to give them a reason to stay until the end. This is done by **opening a loop**, hinting at a payoff that comes later in the video.

- **The Strategy:** Tease a specific **bonus**, a surprising result, or a mistake to avoid that you will reveal later. This creates an **itch** that the viewer can only scratch by finishing the video.
- **Example:** "I'll show you the $5 tool that fixes this, but more importantly, I'm going to show you the one mistake most people make that actually makes the leak worse." (The viewer now has to stay to find out what that mistake is).

3. Introduce the Vibe

Your hook isn't just about information; it's about energy. In 2026, viewers stay for the **vibe** (your personality, your editing style, your background). Use these first moments to show them what it **feels** like to hang out on your channel. If your channel is high-energy, start with a bang. If it's a calm study channel, start with a peaceful, high-quality visual.

The goal of your hook is simple: make it harder for the viewer to leave than it is to stay.

Your Action Steps for Today

1. Write one hook for each of your planned videos. Try different styles: a question, a benefit, or a short personal statement.

2. Read them out loud. Adjust the wording until they sound natural in your voice.

3. Test the hook + introduction timing. Aim to keep your combined hook and introduction under **twenty to twenty-five seconds** for long-form videos. You don't need the perfect opening. You need an opening that respects the viewer's time.

Optional Reflection

Which type of hook feels most natural for you to say out loud? Which hooks make *you* stop scrolling when you watch YouTube videos?

Tomorrow, we'll focus on what happens **after the hook** and how to keep viewers watching through pacing, structure, and simple editing choices that make videos feel dynamic without being overwhelming.

Day 17: Retention Basics for Modern YouTube

You've planned your videos and learned how to hook viewers at the beginning of your video. Now comes the part that decides whether people actually **stay**. Retention on YouTube refers to how long viewers stay and continue watching your video before clicking away. Retention isn't about flashy effects or constant stimulation. It's about how smoothly your video moves, how clearly ideas connect, and how easy it feels to keep watching. Today is about learning the fundamentals of **pacing, structure, and flow**, the quiet skills that separate videos people abandon from videos people finish.

What Retention Really Means

Explained simply, retention is how long viewers stay with your video, and it is something YouTube values particularly. It checks whether:

- People keep watching after the hook.
- They drop off halfway through.
- They make it to the end.

Good retention tells YouTube (and viewers) that your video respects and is worth their time. The biggest factor in retention isn't what you say; it's **how smoothly you say it**.

Understanding Pacing (Without Overthinking It)

Pacing is the rhythm of your video: how fast it moves and how naturally one idea leads to the next.

- Too slow → viewers drift away.
- Too fast → viewers feel overwhelmed.
- Just right → viewers forget to click away.

Good pacing feels steady, intentional, and focused.

Simple Ways to Improve Pacing

You don't need advanced editing skills to tighten your videos. Start here:

- **Cut dead space:** Remove long pauses, repeated phrases, and **thinking moments**. Silence slows momentum.
- **Use jump cuts confidently:** Cutting between parts of the same clip is normal on YouTube. It keeps the energy up and attention locked in.
- **Stay on one idea at a time:** Finish a thought before moving on. Avoid side tangents (distractions or unrelated stories that pop into your head while you are talking about something else) early on.
- **Change something visually every few seconds.** This can be as simple as:
  - A cut to a closer angle.
  - A text label.
  - A quick B-roll clip.
- **Match your speaking energy to the platform:** Slightly more energy than everyday conversation works well; clear and engaged, not rushed.

Structure Creates Flow

Structure is the invisible framework that makes a video's pacing feel effortless. It ensures that each moment leads naturally into the next without losing the viewer's attention. By organizing your ideas into a logical sequence before you hit record, you prevent unnecessary distractions and give your audience a clear, smooth path to follow from your opening hook to your final conclusion.

A simple structure keeps viewers oriented:

- What is this about?
- Where is this going?
- Why should I keep watching?

Even casual videos benefit from:

- Clear sections.
- Logical progression.

- Gentle reminders of what's coming next.

When viewers aren't confused about what to expect, they stay longer.

Visual Storytelling: B-roll and On-Screen Text

Once you have your main footage, it is time to think about how you can keep your viewers' eyes glued to the screen. Two of the most effective tools in your kit are **B-roll** and **on-screen text.** When used correctly, these aren't just decorations; they are the **connective tissue** that helps your audience understand and remember your message.

Creative B-roll Ideas for Beginners

If you are worried about what to show on screen while you speak, remember that **B-roll** is simply there to act as a **visual aid**. Here are a few simple ways to get started:

- **Show the Product:** If you mention a specific item, like a camera or a book, hold it up or show a close-up shot of it. This bridges the gap between what the viewer hears and what they see.
- **Share Your Screen:** If you are teaching someone how to use a website or a piece of software, a simple screen recording is the most helpful thing you can provide. It's like letting the viewer look over your shoulder while you work.
- **Capture the Process:** People love seeing behind the scenes. Footage of you writing in a notebook, typing on your laptop, or setting up your equipment adds a human touch to your video.
- **Use Simple Stock Clips:** You don't always have to film everything yourself. High-quality, free stock clips (pre-recorded video footage made available for public use without cost, often covering generic scenes like nature, cityscapes, or people working) can help break up **talking-head** shots (videos where it is just you speaking to the camera) and keep the visual pace interesting.

The golden rule for **B-roll** is to ensure it supports your words rather than distract from them. If the footage doesn't help explain the point you are currently making, it is probably better to leave it out.

Using On-Screen Text with Purpose

Text is another powerful way to boost **retention**, which is just a fancy way of saying it helps your viewers remember what they learned. However, text should be used with a specific purpose in mind. It works best when it highlights a key phrase, lists the tools you are using, or reinforces a step-by-step process. To keep your video looking professional, remember these three guidelines for text:

1. **Keep it Short:** Use only the most important words.
2. **Make it Readable:** Use a clean font and a color that stands out against your background.
3. **Use it Occasionally:** If every single sentence appears on the screen, nothing will feel important.

As it is said, "If everything is emphasized, then nothing is." Use text like a highlighter pen; only use it on the parts you really want your audience to take home with them.

Audio Matters More Than You Think

Retention drops fast when the audio feels uncomfortable. Quick checks:

- Your voice should always be the loudest element.
- Background music should be subtle.
- Music should match the mood of the video.

Small sound effects (like **light whooshes**) can add energy, but only if they fit your style. When in doubt, keep the audio simple.

A Quick Reminder on YouTube AI Editing (Especially for Shorts)

For Shorts, YouTube's AI editing tools can help with:

- Trimming silences automatically.
- Improving pacing through quick cuts.
- Adding captions that keep viewers engaged.

Use AI to create a **first draft**, then adjust manually. Retention improves when videos still feel human.

Your Action Steps for Today

1. Rehearse one video outline out loud. Notice where you ramble or lose momentum.

2. Film a short segment and edit for flow. Trim pauses, tighten phrasing, and add one visual change if helpful.

3. Watch the edit once as a viewer. Ask yourself: "Would I keep watching this?"

Optional Reflection

Which pacing style feels right for you right now: clean and minimal, energetic and fast, or calm and conversational? What kind of videos do *you* enjoy watching all the way through?

Tomorrow, we'll focus on **titles and thumbnails** and how to earn the click before retention even begins.

Day 18: Titles & Thumbnails as Promises

You can make an excellent video and still get zero views. Not because the content is bad, but because no one clicked. Your **title and thumbnail** are the first impression. Together, they act as a promise to the viewer: "If you click this, here's what you'll get." When that promise is clear, honest, and intriguing, people stop scrolling. Today is about learning how to make titles and thumbnails that **work together**, feel authentic, and earn clicks without exaggeration.

What Titles and Thumbnails Actually Do

Think of them as a pair:

- **Thumbnail = the visual signal.**

It catches attention and creates curiosity.

- **Title = the verbal promise.**

It explains why the video is worth watching. If either one is weak, or if they repeat the same thing, the click often doesn't happen.

Good titles and thumbnails:

When you think about your titles and thumbnails, try not to view them as mere decorations or **extra** chores to finish after you have edited your video. Instead, think of them as your most important strategic tools. These two elements work together like a movie poster and a headline, performing several vital jobs at once to help your channel grow.

First and foremost, a great title-and-thumbnail combination sets clear expectations. It tells the viewer exactly what they are going to get, which helps you attract the right audience, people who are actually interested in your specific topic. When your **packaging** is honest and inviting, it naturally improves your **click-through rate (CTR)**. Just a quick reminder, CTR is the percentage of people who see your video while browsing and decide to click on it; a higher number simply means your **front door** is doing a great job of welcoming people in.

Most importantly, these elements help YouTube understand your content. The platform's systems look at your titles and thumbnails to figure out what your video is about, which allows YouTube to show your work to the people most likely to enjoy it. By being intentional with your choices, you are essentially giving the platform a map to find your future community.

What Makes a Strong Thumbnail

A strong thumbnail communicates **one clear idea** at a glance. It should:

- Be readable on a small screen.
- Focus on a single subject or emotion.
- Match the tone of your content.
- Spark curiosity without misleading.

Beginner-friendly thumbnail styles that consistently work:

- **Face + minimal text:** A clear expression plus a few bold words that hint at the topic.
- **Before/After or Contrast:** Showing change visually (problem → solution).
- **Zoomed-in object or detail:** Great for tutorials, reviews, or explanations.
- **Minimal text-only designs:** Works well for educational or advice-based channels.

You don't need complex design. You need **clarity and contrast**.

Simple Thumbnail Design Guidelines

You don't need professional software. Free tools with templates are more than enough. Beginner-friendly options include **Canva**, which offers YouTube thumbnail templates sized correctly and easy drag-and-drop editing; **Adobe Express**, which works similarly with quick layouts and text tools; and **Pixlr**, a lightweight browser-based editor for simple adjustments.

These tools let you focus on clarity and contrast rather than design skills, which is exactly what matters most for thumbnails.

Keep these basics in mind:

- Use high-resolution images at **1280 × 720 pixels** in a **16:9 widescreen format**, which is the standard size YouTube uses for thumbnails.
- Limit the text to **two to five large words.**
- Use bold fonts and strong contrast.
- Avoid clutter; less is easier to read.
- Make faces expressive if you include them.
- Use files under **2 MB**, which is YouTube's maximum recommended thumbnail file size for uploading without compression issues.

Thumbnails are one of the easiest things to change later, so don't treat them as permanent.

What Makes a Strong Title

If the thumbnail stops the scroll, the title seals the deal. **A good title is:**

- Clear and benefit-driven (meaning the title highlights what the viewer will gain by watching).
- Easy to read (ideally under sixty to seventy characters).
- Focused on one main idea.
- Honest about what the video delivers.

Title formats that work well:

- **How-to:** "How to Plan Your First YouTube Videos"
- **List:** "5 Mistakes New Creators Make"
- **Outcome-focused:** "This Simple Change Improved My Retention"
- **Curiosity-based:** "Why Most Videos Lose Viewers After Thirty Seconds"

- **Personal experience:** "I Tried This for Thirty Days: Here's What Happened"

Ask yourself:

- What problem does this video help solve?
- What curiosity does it trigger?
- Why should someone watch **this** instead of another video?

If your title answers one of those clearly, you're on the right track.

How Title and Thumbnail Should Work Together

Your title and thumbnail should **complement**, not repeat, each other.

- If the title is clear and direct, let the thumbnail be emotional or visual.
- If the title is curiosity-driven, let the thumbnail provide context.

Together, they should create a gap that makes the viewer want to click.

Example 1:

- **Thumbnail**: Surprised face + "4,000 Watch Hours"
- **Title:** "Get 4,000 Watch Hours EASY (Proven Strategy)"

Example 2

• **Thumbnail**: Before vs. After Visuals

• **Title:** "How to Lose Weight in Sixty Days"

Each does a different job but points to the same promise.

Curiosity Gaps: Why We Can't Help but Click

The battle for attention on YouTube isn't won by shouting the loudest; it's won by being the most intriguing. The most effective way to do this is by creating a **curiosity gap.** A curiosity gap is the psychological space between what a viewer knows and what they **want** to know. It's based on **Information Gap Theory**, which suggests that when we notice a gap in our knowledge, it feels like a mental **itch** that we have to scratch. Strong titles and thumbnails raise a specific question in the viewer's mind without answering it fully, making the click feel like the only way to satisfy that curiosity.

How to Build the Gap

- **The Incomplete Visual:** your thumbnail can show the result or the problem, but not the process. If you are fixing a broken sink, show the water spraying everywhere and the finished, sparkling result, not the wrench in the middle of the work.
- **The Open-Ended Title:** Avoid titles that tell the whole story.
    - Weak: "How I Saved $500 by Switching My Phone Plan" (The answer is already in the title).
    - Strong: "The Simple Switch That Saved Me $500" (Now the viewer has to click to find out what the switch was).
- **The "Unexpected" Pairing:** Place two things together that don't seem to fit. This forces the brain to ask, "Wait, why are those two things in the same frame?"
    - Example: A **brand new iPhone 17** being used as a **hammer** for a nail.

The Golden Rule: Don't Tease What You Can't Deliver

The curiosity gap is a **promise**. If your thumbnail asks a question, your video **must** answer it early. If the viewer feels tricked (clickbait), they will leave immediately, which hurts your retention and tells the algorithm your video isn't worth recommending. Now you can try **YouTube's A/B testing** to test which thumbnail and title create the biggest curiosity gaps and lead to people clicking on your video.

Using YouTube A/B Testing for Titles & Thumbnails

In 2026, YouTube allows creators to **test different titles and thumbnails** to see which performs better. A/B testing shows **different versions** of your title or thumbnail to different viewers. YouTube then measures which version gets more clicks and engagement. This removes guesswork and helps you learn what actually works for your audience.

How to Use A/B Testing (Beginner-Friendly)

1. Go to **YouTube Studio**.
2. Select a video (new or existing).
3. Enable A/B testing for:
   - Two thumbnail versions, or
   - Two title versions.
4. Let the test run for a set period.
5. Review the results and keep the stronger version.

You don't need to test everything. Even testing **one small change**, like wording or image style, can teach you a lot.

What to Test First

If you're new, start simple:

- Same thumbnail, different title.
- Same title, different thumbnail.

Avoid changing both at once at the beginning. You want to learn what works and why it works. A/B testing is not about chasing perfection. It's about **learning faster**.

Your Action Steps for Today

1. Create one title + thumbnail pair. Use a simple, proven format. Focus on clarity, not cleverness.

2. Preview them together. Ask yourself: Would I click this if it wasn't my video?

3. Set up A/B testing. Test two versions and let real viewers decide.

Optional Reflection

What titles and thumbnails make you stop scrolling? What patterns do you notice in creators you already enjoy watching?

Tomorrow, we'll move into **discoverability**, how to help YouTube understand your video so it can reach the right audience through search and recommendations.

Day 19: Descriptions, Keywords, and Signals That Matter in 2026

By now, you've done the visible work: filming, editing, titles, and thumbnails. Today is about the **invisible layer**, the signals that help **YouTube** understand your video and decide where and to whom it should be shown. This isn't about gaming the system or stuffing keywords everywhere. In 2026, YouTube SEO is about **clarity**. The clearer your signals, the easier it is for YouTube to match your video with the right viewers.

What YouTube SEO Really Is (In Plain Terms)

YouTube **SEO** (Search Engine Optimization) is the process of helping YouTube understand what your video is about so it can show it to the right people. YouTube functions like a search engine. People type questions and topics into the search bar every day: **how to edit videos, beginner workouts, budget camera reviews.** Your goal is to use clear titles, descriptions, and keywords so YouTube can match your video to those searches. Your job is to **label your video clearly** so YouTube knows:

- What the video is about.
- Who might be interested.
- When it should be suggested.

Good **SEO** won't magically make a bad video popular, but it will help good videos get discovered, especially over time. This is particularly important for **evergreen content**, videos that stay useful months or years after publishing.

Where YouTube Looks for Meaning

YouTube pulls information from multiple places to understand your video, including:

- Your **title.**
- Your **description.**
- Your **tags.**

- Your **spoken words** (auto-captions are scanned).
- Your **uploaded captions** (if you add them).
- Your **file name** (minor, but helpful).

You don't need to optimize everything perfectly. You just need **to be consistent** across these areas.

Writing a Strong Video Description

Think of your description as a clear explanation for both viewers and YouTube.

A solid description has three simple parts:

1. Opening Summary (Most Important). On YouTube, your video description is actually divided into two parts by the **Show More** button. The first two lines are the most valuable, as viewers see them without pressing the **show more** button. To best utilize these first two lines, focus on three simple things:

- Clearly explain what the video covers.
- Use your main keyword naturally.
- Be direct and human.

Example: "In this video, I show beginners how to plan their first YouTube videos, including long-form content and Shorts."

2. Helpful Context and Details. While the first two lines of your description are designed to grab attention, the rest of the space (third line onwards) is for **reinforcing your context.** This is where you provide the roadmap for your video and the resources your viewers need to take the next step. Once a viewer clicks on **Show More,** they should find a well-organized layout that includes:

- Expansion on what's covered.
- Timestamps or Chapters (covered below).
- Link to tools or related videos.

Remember, the goal of this section is **clarity, not repetition.** You aren't just saying the same thing again; you are providing the **meat** of the information that supports your video's message.

Example: "In this video, we cover how to choose your first video topics, how to structure long-form videos, and how Shorts can support your main content. This is part of a beginner-friendly YouTube series focused on building a channel step by step.

00:00 Why your first videos matter

01:12 Choosing your first video topics

04:30 Planning long-form vs Shorts

07:10 Common beginner mistakes"

3. Simple Call to Action (CTA). The end of your description is the perfect place for a **soft landing**. After providing the value and the details, you want to give your viewers a clear, gentle nudge on what to do next. A good closing CTA should achieve one of three things:

- Invite comments.
- Suggest another video.
- Encourage subscribing if the content helped.

Example: "If you're just starting out, let me know in the comments what your channel is about."

Descriptions don't need to be long, but they should be **useful and clear**.

Understanding Tags

As you are finishing up your video details, you might wonder about **tags.** It is a common mistake to look for them in the description box, but they actually live in their own special section. To find them, you will need to scroll all the way to the bottom of your video's **Details** page in YouTube Studio and click on **Show More.** There, you will find a dedicated box where you can type in specific keywords. It is important to know that tags are much less powerful than they once were. Years ago, they were a primary way people found videos, but today, YouTube is much smarter at understanding your content by simply **listening** to your video and reading your title.

However, you can still use tags to:

- Reinforce your main topic.
- Include alternative phrasing.
- Catch common misspellings.
- Add both broad and specific terms.

Example:

- "#youtubeseobeginner"
- "#howtowriteyoutubedescriptions"
- "#videokeywordstutorial"
- Misspellings or variations if relevant.

Aim for **five to ten focused tags**. Avoid unrelated tags; they confuse the system and can hurt performance.

Small Signals That Still Help

These won't make or break a video, but they add clarity.

File Names

Rename your video before uploading. Instead of VID_0423.mp4, use something descriptive like:

how_to_plan_youtube_videos_for_beginners.mp4.

Setting Up Your Captions for Success

When you reach the final stages of preparing your video, it is easy to overlook **captions,** but they are one of the most powerful tools for growing your reach. Captions are not just for viewers who are hard of hearing; they are a vital part of how YouTube's system **reads** your video to understand exactly what you are talking about.

To manage your captions, you won't look in the description box. Instead, while you are in the **Video Details** page of **YouTube Studio**, look at the menu on the right-hand side (near where you choose your thumbnail). You will see a dedicated **Subtitles** or **Captions** section. Once you open that menu, you have a few ways to ensure your video is accessible and easy for the system to understand:

- **Review Your Auto-Captions:** YouTube is quite smart and will often generate **Automatic captions** for you using speech recognition. However, these can sometimes make funny or confusing mistakes. It is a great habit to quickly read through them and fix any errors, especially regarding brand names or technical terms.
- **Upload Your Own File:** If you wrote a script beforehand, you can actually upload that text file directly. YouTube will then sync your words to the timing of your speech. This is often the most accurate way to ensure your message is perfectly preserved.
- **Strengthen Your Signals:** Think of your video like a conversation with the YouTube algorithm. When you have **clear speech** combined with **accurate captions**, you are sending a very strong, clear **signal** about your topic. This makes it much easier for YouTube to recommend your video to the right people.

By taking these few extra minutes, you are making your content more **accessible**, meaning more people can enjoy it, including those watching in noisy places without headphones, while also giving your video a better chance to be discovered.

Using Research Tools (Without Overcomplicating It)

One of the most encouraging things about starting your YouTube journey today is that you never have to guess what might interest people. Instead of wondering if your ideas will resonate, you can use the wealth of data at your fingertips to see exactly what topics your future viewers are already searching for and the specific questions they are hoping to have answered.

Helpful tools include:

- **TubeBuddy:** A browser extension that shows keyword ideas, search volume, and competition directly inside YouTube. You can

use it to test different keyword phrases, see how competitive they are, and optimize your title, description, and tags while uploading.
- **VidIQ:** Another browser-based tool that helps with keyword research and SEO scoring. It shows how often terms are searched, suggests related keywords, and highlights trends so you can choose phrases that are realistic for a new channel.
- **YouTube's own search bar:** Start typing your topic into the YouTube search bar and pay attention to the autocomplete suggestions. These are real queries from real users. Use the wording you see there to shape your titles, descriptions, and tags naturally.

These tools help you:

- See search volume.
- Discover phrasing people actually use.
- Avoid overly competitive keywords early on.

Choose keywords that fit your video naturally. SEO works best when it feels **invisible** to the viewer.

What SEO Can, and Can't, Do

SEO helps YouTube understand what your content is about, show your video to the right audience, and keep evergreen videos discoverable long after they're published. However, it can't fix weak retention, replace strong titles and thumbnails, or force people to keep watching if the video isn't engaging. Think of SEO as support rather than a shortcut. It helps your content get found, but the quality of the idea, packaging, and delivery is what makes people stay.

Bonus: Adding Timestamps (Chapters) to Long-Form Videos

Timestamps, also called **chapters**, help viewers navigate long videos by jumping directly to the part they care about. They improve viewer experience, increase watch time, and make your content feel more professional and organized. This small gesture shows your audience that you value their time, which is a wonderful way to build a loyal community.

In 2026, YouTube can **automatically generate chapters** for many videos, but manual timestamps still give you more control and clarity.

To set these up yourself, follow these simple steps:

1. **Open Your Description Box**: Head into the **Video Details** page in YouTube Studio where you usually write your video description.
2. **Start at the Very Beginning:** This is the most important rule. You must start your list with **00:00** so YouTube knows where the chapters begin. If you skip this, the chapters won't appear on the video player.
3. **Create Your List**: On a new line, type the time code followed by a simple, clear label for that section.

To give you an idea of what this looks like in practice, your list might look something like this:

• 00:00 Introduction

• 01:12 Why this topic matters

• 03:45 Step-by-step walkthrough

• 07:20 Final thoughts and summary

By taking just a minute to organize your description this way, you make your content much more approachable and professional, especially for beginners who might be looking for one specific answer within your video.

Using automatic chapters (YouTube's AI feature):

If you find yourself short on time or have a very long video to organize, you might want to try **Automatic Chapters**. This is a clever feature powered by YouTube's artificial intelligence that attempts to do the organizational work for you.

- YouTube may auto-generate chapters based on your spoken content.
- These appear automatically if the system detects clear structure.
- You can turn them **on or off** in YouTube Studio under: Video → Details → Show more → Allow automatic chapters

Best practice for beginners is to add manual timestamps, even though automatic chapters already exist. They're especially helpful for tutorials, educational videos, longer explanations that run eight minutes or more, and podcasts or interviews where viewers may want to jump to specific sections.

Manual timestamps give you full control over the wording so your labels are clear and human-friendly, allow you to match each section neatly to your outline, and help you avoid confusing or vague AI-generated chapter titles. Think of timestamps as a simple roadmap for your viewer. When people can easily navigate your video and find what they need, they feel more in control and are far more likely to stay longer instead of scrubbing around or clicking away.

Your Action Steps for Today

1. Write a full description for one video. Include a clear opening summary, helpful context, and a simple CTA.

2. Choose five to ten relevant tags. Focus on accuracy and clarity, not volume.

3. Rename your video file (optional but helpful). Use a descriptive, keyword-based name before uploading.

Extra tip: Search your topic on YouTube and study the top results. Notice patterns in wording, not to copy, but to understand what viewers expect.

Optional Reflection

Does your description clearly explain what your video delivers? If you were a new viewer, would it make sense immediately?

Tomorrow, we'll walk through the **upload and publish process**, from choosing the right settings to confidently hitting **Publish** for the first time.

Day 20: What to Check Before Publishing

This is the moment everything has been leading to. You've planned, filmed, edited, written titles and descriptions, and designed a thumbnail. Now it's time to turn all of that work into something real by **uploading your first video**. Feeling nervous is normal. Almost everyone hesitates before their first publication. What matters isn't how polished the video is; it's that you finish the process and learn how publishing actually works. Today is about removing uncertainty so you can click **Publish** with confidence.

Before You Upload: Do a Quick Prep Check

Uploading is much easier when everything is ready in advance. Before you open YouTube Studio, make sure you have:

- Your edited video file (MP4 works best).
- Your custom thumbnail saved as a JPG or PNG and smaller than 2 Mb.
- Your title written and ready.
- Your description drafted.
- A short list of relevant tags.
- A plan for end screens or cards (we will discuss this near the end of this chapter).

Having these ready prevents last-minute second-guessing.

The Upload Process (Step by Step)

Here's how publishing works inside YouTube:

1. Go to YouTube and click **Create (+).**
2. Select **Upload video.**
3. Drag and drop your video file.
4. Fill in the core details:
    - **Title:** Clear, accurate, and aligned with your thumbnail.
    - **Description:** Short summary first, then extra context.
    - **Thumbnail:** Upload your custom image.
5. Choose your audience setting

    - Most creators select **No, not made for kids** unless the video is specifically for children.
6. Add tags and choose a relevant category.
7. Upload captions or review auto-captions (optional but helpful).
8. Select visibility (**Public**, **Unlisted**, or **Private**).
9. Publish immediately or schedule for later.
10. (Optional) Add **end screens** and cards.

Take your time the first time through. As you keep uploading, you will become more familiar and efficient at each step.

Understanding Visibility Settings

YouTube gives you three main options:

- **Public:** The video is live and discoverable immediately.
- **Unlisted:** The video is viewable only via direct link. It's great for previews or sharing privately.
- **Private:** Only you (or selected people) can see the video. It's useful for drafts or tests.

If this is your first upload and you're nervous, **Unlisted** is a perfectly valid first step.

Tip: Before publishing, run through your personal upload checklist or the *bonus section's Video Production Checklist for YouTube* to make sure nothing is missed.

How Long Publishing Takes (What to Expect)

When you click **Publish**, your video usually becomes visible on your channel **within seconds**. However, full availability across YouTube can take a little longer.

Here's what's normal:

- **Public videos:** Appear on your channel almost immediately but may take **a few minutes to an hour** to fully show up in search, recommendations, and subscription feeds.

- **Scheduled videos:** Go live automatically at the scheduled time and date, often within a minute or two.
- **Unlisted videos:** They are viewable right away using the link but don't appear publicly.
- **Private videos:** Are visible only to you (or selected users) until you change the setting.

In some cases, YouTube may take longer to process and show your video due to:

- HD or 4K quality (the higher the quality, the more time it takes).
- Content checks for copyright or advertiser safety.
- Heavy traffic or system processing delays.

This is normal and not a sign that something went wrong.

Important: One thing that often surprises new creators is that your video isn't **finished** the moment the upload bar hits 100%. You might notice that when you first view your live video, the picture quality looks a bit blurry or grainy. Don't worry, this doesn't mean you made a mistake during filming or editing! What is happening behind the scenes is simply YouTube processing your video. When you upload a video, YouTube's first priority is to make it available to watch as quickly as possible. To do this, it creates a low-quality version (known as **Standard Definition** or **SD**) first. While your viewers can start watching this version immediately, YouTube is still working hard in the background to build the high-quality, crisp versions (like 1080p or 4K).

End Screens: A Small Feature with Big Impact

End screens appear in the final five to twenty seconds of your video and can:

- Suggest another video or playlist.
- Encourage subscriptions.
- Guide viewers to what's next.

Even a simple **Subscribe** end screen helps build habits for future videos.

How to add end screens:

1. Go to **YouTube Studio.**
2. Select **Content**, then click on the video you want to edit.
3. Open the **Editor** tab in the left menu.
4. Click on **End screen.**
5. Choose what you want to add (video, playlist, subscribe button, or channel).
6. Position the elements within the last five to twenty seconds of your video.
7. Preview, then **Save.**

Start simple. One **end screen** element is enough for your first few videos.

The Finishing Touches: Don't Skip These Small Settings

As you reach the final screen before your video goes live, it is easy to feel a rush to hit **Publish** and be done. However, taking just sixty seconds to check a few small settings can make a huge difference in how people discover and interact with your work. Think of these as the final **quality checks** that ensure your video is organized and ready for guests.

Organizing with Playlists

One of the best ways to keep viewers watching your content is to use **playlists.** A playlist is simply a collection of videos grouped by a specific theme. I highly recommend adding your video to a playlist if it fits into a series or a broader topic. For example, if you are making a series of "Cooking for Beginners" videos, putting them all in one place allows a viewer to finish one and automatically start the next.

If you haven't created one yet, don't worry; it is very simple to do right from the upload screen:

- In the **Video Details** section, look for the **Playlists** dropdown menu.
- If you don't see a suitable category, click **New Playlist**.
- Give it a clear, descriptive title that tells people what the collection is about, and hit **Create**.

By grouping your videos this way, you are making it much easier for someone who likes one of your videos to **binge-watch** your entire library.

Encouraging a Conversation in the Comments

YouTube is a social platform, and the **Comments** section is where your community starts to form. I suggest leaving your comments turned **On** unless you have a very specific reason to keep them closed. Hearing from your viewers is the best way to learn what they like and what they want to see next.

To ensure your comments are active, scroll down to the bottom of your settings page in YouTube Studio and click **Show More.** Under the **Comments and ratings** section, you can choose how you want to handle feedback. Most creators choose **Hold potentially inappropriate comments for review**, which allows the friendly conversations to appear immediately while giving you a chance to filter out anything that doesn't belong on your channel.

A Final Look at the Monetization Tab

If you have already reached the milestones to join the **YouTube Partner Program (YPP)**, you will also see a **Monetization** tab. Here, you can decide if you want ads to play during your video. We are going to dive deep into exactly how this works and how you get paid in a later chapter, so for now, just know that this is the place where you **turn on the lights** for your channel's earnings.

What Happens After You Publish

Once you click on Publish, YouTube begins observing how viewers respond:

- Are people clicking? (Title + thumbnail).
- Are they watching? (Retention and pacing).
- Are they engaging? (Likes, comments, watch time).

Your video may appear instantly on your channel, but it can take a little time to fully populate across search, Home, and recommendations.

In some cases, YouTube may run additional checks, especially if:

- Copyrighted music is detected.
- Monetization is enabled.
- Content needs advertiser review. (This simply means YouTube is double-checking your video to ensure it follows their **advertiser-friendly** rules so that brands feel comfortable showing their ads alongside your content).

All of this is normal. You'll be notified in YouTube Studio if anything needs attention.

Perspective Matters Here

Your first video does not need to perform well; it simply needs to exist. Publishing teaches you more than planning ever will. Every upload builds confidence, clarity, and momentum.

Your Action Steps for Today

1. Upload a video. This can be your real first video or a test upload.

2. Apply everything you've prepared. Title, thumbnail, description, tags, and use what you've already built.

3. Choose visibility and publish or schedule. Take a breath and complete the process.

4. Acknowledge the milestone. You've officially become a creator.

Tomorrow, we'll talk about **monetization and copyright basics** and how to protect your channel and set yourself up to earn responsibly as you grow.

Day 21: Copyright, Fair Use, and Monetization Safety

You've uploaded your first video. That alone puts you ahead of most people who never make it past planning. Now it's time to understand something that protects everything you're building: **how monetization works and how to avoid copyright problems before they happen**. This chapter isn't about chasing money quickly. It's about **keeping your channel safe**, eligible, and stress-free as it grows.

How Monetization Works on YouTube (Big Picture)

YouTube allows creators to earn money directly on the platform, but only if their channel follows the rules. Monetization isn't automatic. It unlocks once you qualify for the **YouTube Partner Program (YPP)** and continue following YouTube's policies. Think of monetization as a privilege, not a guarantee. Staying eligible matters more than turning ads on early.

YPP: What You Need in 2026

As mentioned on *Day 6: How YouTube Monetization Works (What to Aim For and Why)*, to apply for monetization, your channel must follow **one** of these paths:

Option 1: Long-Form Videos

- At least **1,000 subscribers.**
- **4,000 valid public watch hours** in the last twelve months (Only public videos and livestreams count).

Option 2: Shorts

- At least **1,000 subscribers.**
- **10 million valid public Shorts views** in the last ninety days.

Once you've met one of these thresholds, you must also:

- Follow **YouTube monetization policies.**
- Have an approved **AdSense account**.

Once approved, you will unlock ads, memberships, Super Thanks, and more (covered later in the guide).

How to Turn Monetization On for a Video

You can enable or change monetization at two points:

During Upload

1. Go to **YouTube Studio.**
2. Click on **Create (+) → Upload video.**
3. Upload your video and move through the setup screens.
4. When you reach the **Monetization** step:
   - Toggle **Monetization ON.**
   - Select the ad formats you want to allow. (The different **ad formats** are explained below).
5. Complete the **ad suitability self-check.** (This is a simple but important process that is explained in detail below).
6. Continue and publish or schedule.

After a Video Is Published

1. Open **YouTube Studio.**
2. Go to **Content.**
3. Click on the video you want to edit.
4. Select the **Monetization** tab.
5. Toggle monetization **on or off.**
6. Adjust ad formats if needed.
7. Save changes.

You can change these settings at any time.

Understanding Each Ad Type

Skippable Ads

- Play before or during the video.
- Viewers can skip after five seconds.
- Revenue is earned if viewers watch long enough or interact.

Why they matter: These are the most common and viewer-friendly ads. They balance revenue with audience experience and are recommended for most creators.

Non-Skippable Ads

- Short ads (usually six to fifteen seconds).
- Must be watched in full before the video continues.
- Typically earn more per view.

Important note: While they can pay more, too many non-skippable ads may frustrate viewers. YouTube often limits how frequently these appear.

Display / Banner Ads

- Appear beside or below the video (mostly on desktop).
- Do not interrupt playback.
- Generate income when clicked.

Best for: Passive monetization without affecting watch time or viewer experience.

Mid-Roll Ads (Videos over eight minutes)

- Appear in the middle of longer videos.
- Can be placed automatically by YouTube or manually by you.

Best practices:

- For your videos that are over eight minutes long, place mid-rolls at natural breaks (topic changes, pauses) or before the reveal.
- Avoid placing them mid-sentence or mid-thought.
- Fewer, well-placed mid-rolls usually perform better than many poorly placed ones.

When used thoughtfully, mid-roll ads can significantly increase revenue on long-form content.

The Ad Suitability Self-Check

When you are ready to turn on monetization, you will encounter the **Ad Suitability Self-Check**. This is not a section you should rush through or skip, as it is essentially a **trust exercise** between YouTube and yourself.

Instead of relying solely on automated systems to guess what is in your video, YouTube asks you to provide an honest rating of your own content. This helps the platform place the right ads on your video much faster. During this check, you will be asked to rate your video based on a few key categories:

- **Language:** Does your video contain any **profanity** or **strong** language?
- **Topics Discussed:** Are you covering **sensitive subjects** or controversial issues?
- **Imagery:** Does your video show any **graphic violence** or adult-themed visuals?
- **Sensitive Material:** Is there anything that might be considered harmful or inappropriate for certain audiences?

It is vital to always answer these questions with complete honesty. Being transparent about your content actually protects your channel in the long run. If the system frequently finds that your self-rating doesn't match the actual content, a situation known as **mislabeling**, it can lead to some frustrating setbacks. You might face **demonetization** after the video is already live, experience unexpected manual reviews that delay your earnings, or see a reduction in the **trust score** YouTube assigns to your channel. By taking an extra moment to be accurate now, you are ensuring your monetization remains stable and your relationship with the platform stays strong.

A Beginner-Friendly Monetization Approach

If you're unsure which ads to choose:

- Start with **skippable ads** and **display ads.**
- Add **mid-roll ads** once your videos are longer and structured.
- Let YouTube handle placement at first, then refine later.

Revenue tends to grow gradually, and it almost always follows viewer trust rather than precedes it. Monetization isn't about squeezing every dollar out of every video. It's about building a channel that stays **eligible, watchable, and sustainable**.

Copyright: Where Most New Creators Get Stuck

Copyright issues are one of the fastest ways to lose monetization or your channel. **Copyright** means the legal ownership of creative work (such as music, videos, images, or artwork). If you use someone else's protected content without their permission or a proper license, the owner has the right to claim, block, or remove your video. Even accidental use can trigger problems.

Common Copyright Triggers

- Music you don't own (even a few seconds).
- Movie, TV, or anime clips.
- Footage from other creators.
- Images, artwork, or graphics without credit.
- Background music picked up while filming in public.

YouTube's Content ID system is extremely good at detection, even background audio.

Copyright Claims vs Copyright Strikes

When you are first starting out, seeing a **Copyright** notification can be scary. However, on YouTube, not all copyright notices entail the same thing. It is very helpful to think of these like sports penalties: one is a **yellow card** warning, while the other is a **red card** that can lead to being kicked out of the game.

Here is the difference explained in simple terms:

The Copyright Claim (The Yellow Card)

A **Copyright Claim** is the most common notice you will see. It usually happens automatically when YouTube's **Content ID** system hears a song or sees a clip in your video that belongs to someone else.

- **What it means:** The owner has identified their work in your video. Most of the time, they aren't angry; they just want to be the one to earn money from that specific video.
- **What happens to you:** Your channel is still in good standing. Your video usually stays live for everyone to see, but any money earned from ads will go to the content owner instead of you. In some cases, the owner might choose to mute the music or block the video in certain countries.
- **The Bottom Line:** It doesn't hurt your channel's future, but it does mean you won't profit from that specific video.

The Copyright Strike (The Red Card)

A **Copyright Strike** is much more serious. This isn't an automatic computer check; it happens when a copyright owner manually tells YouTube that you used their work without permission and asks for your video to be taken down.

- **What it means:** This is a formal legal request. YouTube is required by law to remove your video immediately.
- **What happens to you:** You will receive a **strike** against your channel. Think of this as a mark on your permanent record. You might lose access to certain features, like live streaming, for a short period of time.

- **The Three-Strike Rule:** This is the part to remember. If you get **three strikes** within a ninety-day window, YouTube will permanently delete your channel and all the videos on it. You will also be banned from creating any new channels.
- **The Bottom Line:** Avoiding strikes should be your top priority. While a single strike will expire after ninety days, having one puts your entire channel at risk.

The best way to stay safe is to always use original content or music from the YouTube Audio Library, which we will talk about next.

How to Stay Monetization-Safe

Here are some beginner-friendly rules that protect your channel:

- Use **royalty-free music**. (This simply refers to music you can use without having to pay a fee (a royalty) every time your video is played).
- Avoid unlicensed clips, even short ones.
- Create original thumbnails and visuals.
- Don't reuse content you didn't create.
- Read licensing terms before using assets.

If you didn't create it or license it, don't use it.

Fair Use: Helpful but Risky

It is time to talk about one of the most misunderstood topics on the platform: **Fair Use**. As a beginner, you will hear this term constantly, often used as if it is a **magic shield** that allows you to use any movie clip or song you want. In reality, **Fair Use** is a bit more complex and a bit more risky than it first appears.

What Exactly Is Fair Use?

At its heart, **Fair Use** is a legal principle that says you can use small portions of someone else's copyrighted work without asking for permission, but only under very specific conditions. It exists to protect your right to express your own ideas, learn, and share information.

Think of it this way: the law wants to protect the original creator, but it also doesn't want to stop you from being a critic, a teacher, or a comedian. Generally, your use of a clip or image is more likely to be considered **fair** if you are using it for:

- **Commentary or Criticism:** You are talking **about** the clip, explaining why it is good, bad, or interesting.
- **Education:** You are using the clip to teach a specific lesson or concept.
- **News Reporting:** You are using the footage to inform the public about a current event.
- **Parody:** You are making fun of the original work in a transformative way.

The Great Catch of YouTube

Here is where many beginners get stuck: **YouTube is not a court of law.** Even if your video perfectly follows the legal rules of **Fair Use**, YouTube's automated **Content ID system** cannot tell the difference between a thoughtful critique and a simple copy.

Because a computer is doing the checking, your video might still receive a copyright claim the moment you upload it. This can lead to your video being temporarily removed, or more commonly, the money earned from your video being sent to the original owner instead of you.

How to Use Fair Use Correctly

If you decide to use copyrighted material under **Fair Use**, you need to be **transformative**. This means you must add something significant and new to the original work. You aren't just **sharing** the clip; you are changing its meaning through your own insight.

To stay as safe as possible, keep these mentor tips in mind:

- **Add Your Voice:** Never let a copyrighted clip play by itself. You

should be talking over it, pausing it to explain a point, or appearing on screen to discuss it.
- **Keep it Short:** Only use as much as you absolutely need to make your point. If a five-second clip proves your point, don't use thirty seconds.
- **Provide Context:** Your audience (and the copyright owner) should clearly understand why that clip is there. It should support your words, not replace them.
- **Avoid the Heart of the Work:** Try not to use the most famous or important part of a movie or song (like the **big twist** ending or the catchy chorus), as this makes it harder to argue that your use is fair.

Remember, **Fair Use** is a **legal defense**, not a guarantee. It is a powerful tool for creators, but it requires a careful hand and a lot of respect for the original work. When in doubt, the safest path is always to create your own original visuals or use royalty-free libraries.

Famous Channels That Use Fair Use Successfully

LegalEagle: LegalEagle uses clips from movies, TV shows, and viral videos to explain legal concepts. The clips are always short and are immediately followed by analysis, explanation, or correction. The original material is never the focus; the commentary is. This is a textbook example of educational fair use.

CinemaSins: CinemaSins uses short movie clips paired with constant narration, critique, and humor. The clips are broken up, heavily edited, and never shown in full. The content is transformed into commentary and parody rather than passive viewing

If your content needs to use copyrighted content, you can learn from these channels on how to use fair use successfully.

Music: The #1 Risk Area

Music causes more **copyright issues** than anything else. Fortunately, you have several wonderful ways to find high-quality music that won't put your channel at risk.

- **The YouTube Audio Library:** This is my top recommendation for beginners. It is a free, built-in library inside your YouTube Studio filled with thousands of tracks and sound effects that are pre-cleared for you to use. Since it is owned by YouTube, it is the safest possible choice.
- **Licensed Subscription Platforms:** If you are looking for a more specific sound or want access to a massive library of professional-grade music, you might consider a paid subscription. These platforms handle all the legal licensing for you as part of your monthly fee. Excellent examples include:
  - **Epidemic Sound:** Very popular for its huge variety and easy-to-use search tools.
  - **Artlist:** Known for its cinematic quality and simple, **license-everything** approach.
  - **Musicbed:** A great choice if you are looking for music from real, independent artists that feels less like **stock** music.
- **Original Music:** If you are a musician and you own 100% of the rights to the song you wrote and recorded, you are always safe to use it.

What to Avoid at All Costs

To protect your channel's future, try to stay away from these common traps:

- **Popular Radio Songs:** Even if you only use five seconds of a famous song, the system will likely catch it. Unless you have paid thousands of dollars for a specific license, keep the radio hits out of your videos.
- **Royalty-Free Tracks Without Proof:** Be careful with random websites or YouTube channels that claim music is **Royalty-Free**. If they don't provide a clear, written license or a way to whitelist your channel, you could still end up with a claim later on.
- **Background Music in Public:** If you are filming at a coffee shop or a gym and there is music playing over the speakers in the background, your microphone will pick it up. YouTube's system is often sensitive enough to claim your video based on that background noise, so try to film in quiet areas or mute the original audio in those moments.

By choosing your audio from trusted sources, you can focus on your creativity without the constant worry of a copyright notification popping up in your inbox.

AI Content and Monetization (Good News)

One of the most common questions for new creators in 2026 is whether using **Artificial Intelligence** will hurt their chances of making money. The great news is that YouTube remains a place where technology and creativity can live together. AI-assisted content is fully eligible for monetization, and there is no ban on using these tools to help build your channel.

However, to keep your channel in good standing and ensure your earnings are protected, you need to understand the difference between **using AI as a tool** and **using it as a replacement** for your own voice.

Balancing Innovation with Authenticity

YouTube's primary goal is to reward original, human creativity. If you use AI to simply **mass-produce** hundreds of videos that look and sound exactly the same, the platform may flag that as **repetitive** or **inauthentic** content. To stay on the right side of the rules, focus on these three pillars:

- **Original Value:** Even if an AI helps you write a script or generate an image, the final video should still have your unique **human touch**. This means adding your own commentary, personal stories, humor, or a specific editing style that an AI couldn't create on its own.
- **Policy Compliance:** All AI-generated content must still follow the same rules as every other video. This means avoiding **deepfakes** that impersonate real people without permission or using AI to create harmful or misleading information.
- **Transparency and Labeling:** This is a vital step for creators in 2026. If you use AI to create a scene that looks **completely realistic** but didn't actually happen, like a lifelike AI version of a famous city or a realistic-sounding AI voice for a person, you must disclose this. During the upload process, you will see a setting for

Altered Content where you simply let YouTube know that the footage is synthetic.

When You Don't Need to Worry

You do not need to label your content if the AI is just helping you behind the scenes. Using tools for brainstorming ideas, checking your grammar, or organizing your research is considered **productivity use** and doesn't require any special disclosure.

In short, AI tools are allowed, but policy violations are not. As long as you are using these tools to enhance your own ideas rather than letting a machine do 100% of the work, you are in a great position to grow and monetize your channel.

Your Action Steps for Today

1. Open YouTube Studio → Earn tab. Check your progress toward **YPP** eligibility.

2. Review monetization settings (if eligible). Practice toggling monetization and exploring ad options.

3. Audit your content for copyright risk. Pay close attention to music and visuals.

4. Explore the YouTube Audio Library. Save a few tracks you might use in future videos.

Optional Reflection

Are you prioritizing speed or sustainability? What's one habit you can adopt now to avoid copyright stress later?

Tomorrow, we'll start a new week by looking at **analytics basics:** how to read early data without overreacting and what actually matters after your first uploads.

Week 4: Growth, Income, and Long-Term Strategy

You've built the foundation of your channel. You've published your first videos, learned how the platform works, and crossed the hardest line any creator faces: starting. Now, the focus shifts from simply getting content online to understanding how to grow, earn, and stay consistent over time.

This week is about moving beyond launch mode and into sustainable creation. Instead of asking, "Did this video perform well?" you'll begin learning how to read your analytics calmly and use them as guidance rather than judgment. You'll explore how YouTube actually measures growth, what early numbers mean (and don't mean), and how to improve without chasing every metric.

You'll also start thinking about your audience in a deeper way. Growth on YouTube isn't just about views; it's about trust, familiarity, and community. This week introduces ways to connect with viewers, encourage engagement, and create content that makes people want to come back, not just click once.

Income is part of the conversation too, but with a long-term lens. You'll learn how creators earn beyond ads, how monetization fits into a broader strategy, and how to stay organized as your channel becomes something more than a hobby. This final stretch gives you room to refine your workflow, strengthen your habits, and think intentionally about what comes next. By the end of Week Four, you won't just know how to upload videos; you'll understand how to keep going with clarity, confidence, and balance.

You're not just starting a YouTube channel anymore. You're building a creative system that can grow with you in 2026 and beyond.

A Note for the Road Ahead: As we dive into these more advanced topics, remember that much of what we discuss this week may not be applicable on your very first day. **Don't feel like you have to master or implement everything at once.** It is perfectly normal to feel a bit overwhelmed by the **business side** of YouTube. View these chapters as a roadmap for the future rather than a to-do list for today. Think of this information as a resource you can keep in your back pocket; focus on what helps you right now, and feel free to come back and revisit these strategies whenever you reach a new milestone or feel ready to take the next step.

Day 22: Reading Analytics Without Overthinking Them

Once your videos are live, it's natural to wonder whether they're actually working. Are people clicking? Are they watching? Are they coming back? This is where YouTube Analytics comes in, not as a judgment tool, but as feedback. YouTube Analytics is built directly into **YouTube Studio**, and it gives you real insight into how viewers are interacting with your content. Today is about learning how to read that data calmly, focusing on what matters most, and avoiding spiraling over numbers that don't yet tell the full story.

Why Analytics Matter (Even Early On)

Analytics show you how real people respond to your videos. They answer questions like, "Are viewers clicking when they see your video? Do they stay to watch or leave early? Are they engaging by liking, commenting, or subscribing?" The goal is not to monitor every fluctuation. The goal is to notice patterns over time so you can repeat what works and gently improve what doesn't. Analytics are feedback, not a verdict.

Where to Find Your Analytics

Inside YouTube Studio, click on **Analytics** in the left-hand menu. You'll land on the **Overview** page, which gives you a snapshot of views, watch time, and subscriber changes. From there, you can explore the **Content**, **Audience**, and **Reach** sections. You don't need monetization to access these insights. Performance data is available from your very first upload. The Revenue tab appears only after joining the **YouTube Partner Program (YPP)**, but everything else is already there to help you grow.

The Metrics That Actually Matter for Beginners

- **Views:** Show how many times your video was watched, but don't tell the full story on their own.
- **Watch time:** Measures how long people spend watching your content. This is one of the strongest indicators YouTube uses when deciding whether to recommend a video.

- **Average View Duration (AVD):** Shows how long viewers watch on average. For beginners, aiming for about **40–50% of the total video length** is a solid benchmark. Early drop-offs often point to pacing, structure, or a weak hook.
- **Click-through rate (CTR):** Measures how often people click your video after seeing the title and thumbnail. For new channels, **4–10% is normal**, and anything higher is excellent. CTR reflects how well your video is packaged, not the quality of the content itself. High CTR gets the audience in the door, but high **satisfaction** keeps the door open.
- **Audience retention (the satisfaction check):** Shows exactly where viewers drop off. If your **thirty-second retention** is weak, it usually signals a **mismatch**. This happens when the first thirty seconds didn't deliver what the title and thumbnail promised. In 2026, YouTube optimizes for **viewer satisfaction,** not just views. It looks at CTR, average view duration, and even post-watch surveys to see if you actually made the viewer happy.
- **Top-performing videos:** Reviewing which videos perform best can be very revealing. Look for patterns in topic, structure, length, or tone and apply those insights to future uploads.

A Major 2026 Update: Organic vs Paid Performance

One of the biggest changes for YouTube creators in 2026 is a new feature in your Analytics that separates your video's performance into **two lanes: Organic and Paid**.

To understand why this is a game-changer for your channel, think of your video as a new restaurant.

- **Organic results** are like people walking in because they smelled the food or heard a friend talk about it. This is **word-of-mouth** growth.
- **Paid results** are like people who came in because you handed them a flyer or put up a billboard.

In the past, YouTube mixed all these people together, which made it very hard to see if your **food** (your content) was actually good or if your **flyers** (your ads) were just being handed to the wrong people (we'll talk about paid promotion and ads in the next chapter).

Why This Separation Helps You

Before this update, many creators felt discouraged when they started promoting their videos. They would see their average **watch time** or **click rates** drop and assume their video was failing.

In reality, people who find you organically (naturally) are usually your **super fans** or people specifically looking for your topic. People who see your paid ads are often seeing you for the very first time. Naturally, these new viewers might not stay as long as your loyal fans. Now that these numbers are separated, you can see the truth:

- If your organic numbers are high, your video is great! Your creative idea is a success.
- If your paid numbers are lower, it doesn't mean your video is bad; it just means your ad might need a better **hook** for strangers, or you might need to show it to a different group of people.

How to Use the New Filters

You can find these new toggles right inside the Analytics tab of your YouTube Studio. Look near the top of the page (or inside **Advanced Mode**), and you will see filters for **Organic** and **Paid**.

- Select **Organic**: This shows you only the viewers who found you through search, recommendations, or their subscription feed. This is your true content score.
- Select **Paid**: This shows you only the results from your advertising, such as when you use YouTube Promote.

Reading the Data Without the Stress

The most important thing to remember is that these two numbers aren't supposed to match.

- **Don't panic about Click-Through Rate (CTR):** it is normal for your organic CTR to be higher because those viewers already know and trust you. If your paid CTR is lower, it just means you are reaching a **cold audience** who needs a bit more convincing.

- **Look for patterns, not just high numbers:** instead of comparing your ads to your organic views, compare your new organic results to your old organic results. This helps you see if your content is actually improving over time without the noise of ad data getting in the way.

By looking at these two lanes separately, you can make much smarter decisions about how to grow your channel without the unnecessary stress of confusing averages.

A Note on Timing

In the first twenty-four to forty-eight hours of uploading a video, analytics can look unstable. YouTube often tests new videos with small groups before expanding reach. Give your data time to settle before drawing conclusions.

For a small channel, success isn't defined by an overnight explosion in views, but by the steady accumulation of knowledge and skill. Every upload is a lesson that builds the foundation for the growth that follows.

The Big Three: What to Actually Watch

Don't get lost in the **Advanced Mode** sea of data. When you are just beginning, focus on these three numbers to understand your growth:

1. **Click-Through Rate (CTR):** Did the thumbnail/title promise work?
2. **Average View Duration (AVD):** Did the content deliver on that promise?
3. **Returning Viewers:** This is the ultimate **community** signal. It shows if people liked you enough to come back for more.

Your Action Steps for Today

1. Open YouTube Studio → Analytics. Spend time in the Overview, Content, and Audience tabs without rushing. If you've run promotions before, toggle between organic and paid performance to see how they differ.

2. Choose one metric to improve. Pick a single focus for your next video; CTR, audience retention, or average view duration are great starting points.

3. Study your top-performing video. Look at what's working. Consider the topic, structure, pacing, or title and thumbnail, and note what you can repeat or refine.

Optional Reflection

Do you tend to overcheck numbers or avoid them altogether? How can you use analytics as guidance rather than pressure as you move forward?

Tomorrow, we'll look at how to grow your **audience beyond YouTube itself**, using promotion strategies that actually work without feeling pushy or exhausting.

Day 23: Growing Your Audience With Intentional Promotion

You've uploaded your first videos. That alone puts you ahead of most people who never make it past planning. The next question is the one every new creator asks sooner or later: How do people actually find my videos?

The answer is simple but often misunderstood. YouTube is powerful, but it's not automatic, especially in the beginning. Early growth comes from a mix of **smart promotion, real human sharing, and giving the algorithm clear signals** that your content is worth showing to more people.

Think of YouTube as the stage and your video as the performance. Promotion is how you invite people into the room.

The Upload and Wait Myth

Many beginners believe that if they just upload consistently, YouTube will eventually do the rest. While the algorithm does help over time, it needs data first, and that data comes from viewers interacting with your video.

Early on, most views come from places outside YouTube: people you share the video with, platforms where you already exist, and communities that care about your topic. These early clicks, comments, and watch time help YouTube understand who your video is for.

Choosing Where to Promote (You Don't Need Everything)

You don't need to be on every social media platform to grow. Trying to show up everywhere at once usually leads to burnout and inconsistent promotion. The best place to start is wherever you already feel comfortable and where your ideal viewers already spend time. One or two platforms, used consistently and thoughtfully, will do far more for your channel than spreading yourself thin across five.

Short-form discovery platforms like **Instagram Reels** and **TikTok** are excellent places to introduce new people to your content. These platforms are designed to surface videos to users who don't already follow you, which makes them especially useful for new creators. A short clip pulled from your video, a strong insight, a surprising moment, a clear takeaway, or a relatable line works best as a teaser. You're not trying to explain everything. You're creating curiosity and giving viewers a reason to look you up. A simple call to action like "full video on my channel" is enough.

Platforms like **Facebook and LinkedIn** work best when your content is practical, educational, or niche-specific. Facebook groups can be particularly powerful if you approach them as communities rather than promotion boards. Spend time observing discussions, answering questions, and only share your video when it genuinely adds value. When people discover your content as a helpful resource rather than a dropped link, they're more likely to subscribe and return. LinkedIn performs especially well for tutorials, professional advice, and learning-focused content when paired with a short explanation of who the video is for and why it's useful.

Text-based platforms like **X (formerly Twitter)** are ideal for conversation and idea-sharing. Instead of posting a link on its own, share a short insight or opinion drawn from your video. Threads work well here: break one idea into a few concise points, then offer the video as a deeper dive at the end. This feels natural, low-pressure, and aligned with how people already use the platform.

Pinterest functions less like a social network and more like a visual search engine. This makes it especially valuable for evergreen content, videos that stay relevant over time. Creating pins that link to your YouTube videos allows your content to be discovered weeks or even months after publishing. For niches like food, DIY, productivity, home organization, and learning, Pinterest can quietly become a steady source of traffic with minimal ongoing effort.

How YouTube Shorts Support Long-Form Growth

Even if your main focus is long-form videos, **YouTube Shorts** can play a powerful supporting role. Shorts are not a replacement for long content; they're a discovery tool that helps new viewers find you faster.

Shorts are shown to people who may have never seen your channel before. When someone enjoys a Short, YouTube makes it very easy for them to tap through to your channel, where they can discover your longer videos. This makes Shorts a natural funnel: short content introduces you, and long content builds depth and loyalty.

The most effective Shorts for long-form creators are usually pulled directly from existing videos. A strong hook, a clear tip, a bold statement, or a quick moment of insight works well. You're not summarizing the entire video; you're highlighting one compelling piece that stands on its own while hinting that there's more context in the full version.

Shorts also help train the algorithm more quickly. Because they receive feedback fast through views, watch time, and rewatches, they give YouTube early signals about your content style and the kind of audience it appeals to. Even if a Short doesn't directly drive clicks to a long video, it can still introduce your channel to new viewers who may return later.

The key is intention. Treat Shorts as highlights, not leftovers. Make them clear, engaging, and valuable on their own, while subtly pointing viewers toward your longer content. When used this way, Shorts become one of the easiest ways to grow awareness without doubling your workload.

Promotion works best when everything connects. Long-form videos build trust, Shorts spark discovery, and external platforms widen the door. You don't need to do all of it at once, just enough to help the right people find you.

Email and Direct Sharing Still Matter

If you have an email list, even a small one, this is one of the strongest places to start. These people already chose to hear from you. A simple message saying you've posted a new video and would love their thoughts is more than enough.

If you don't have a list, personal sharing still counts. Sending your video to a few friends or family members who genuinely care can give you early feedback and engagement that helps your confidence and your analytics.

A Major 2026 Update: YouTube Collaborations

One of the most important growth features YouTube has introduced is **Collaborations.** This feature allows you to officially collaborate with other creators directly inside YouTube on both long-form videos and Shorts.

Instead of working in isolation, you can now invite up to five other creators to be **co-authors** of a single video. Here is why this is a game-changer for new channels:

- **Shared Audience:** When you use this feature, the video doesn't just show up on your channel; it appears in the **subscription feeds** of every person you collaborated with. It's like being introduced to five new audiences at the exact same time.
- **One-Tap Subscribing:** Viewers don't have to hunt for your link. All the collaborators' channel names and **Subscribe** buttons appear directly on the video player, making it effortless for new fans to follow you.

By using Collaborations, you aren't just making a video; you are building a network. It's one of the fastest ways to get your content in front of people who already love your niche but just haven't discovered you yet.

Even though you are sharing the spotlight, you never have to worry about losing control of your content. In 2026, YouTube's collaboration system is designed to keep the **lead creator** in the driver's seat.

- **You Keep the Earnings:** All views, watch time, and ad revenue belong strictly to the channel that originally uploaded the video. There are no complicated revenue splits to manage; you remain the sole owner of the **digital asset.**
- **You Manage the Data:** You decide how much information your partners can see. You can grant them **View-Only** access to the video's performance (like how many people are watching and where they are coming from) without giving them access to your private financial data or the rest of your channel.
- **Total Flexibility:** You have the power to manage or remove collaborators at any time. If a partnership ends or you simply want to change how the video is credited, you can update those settings with a few clicks in YouTube Studio.

This setup makes collaborating virtually risk-free. You get the benefit of a massive audience boost while keeping your channel's ownership and income completely secure.

How to Add Collaborators to a YouTube Video (Step by Step)

1. Open **YouTube Studio** on desktop or mobile.
2. Click on **Create (+)** and start uploading a new video or Short.
3. On the **Details** page, select **Show more**.
4. Click on **Invite a collaborator**.
5. Search for the channel you want to collaborate with.
6. Choose whether to allow them to view video analytics (this never includes revenue).
7. Click on **Create link** and send the invite link to your collaborator.
8. Ask your collaborator to open the link and **accept the invite**.
9. Once accepted, the collaboration goes live, and the video appears in both your feed and your collaborators' subscription feeds.

Optional: Feature collaborations on your channel homepage

1. Go to **YouTube Studio → Customization → Home tab**.
2. Click on **Add section**.
3. Choose **Collaborations**.
4. Save your changes so visitors immediately see your joint videos.

This turns collaboration into a built-in growth engine. You're not just hoping someone shares your video; you're structurally placing your content in front of new, relevant audiences.

Why Collaboration Works So Well

Collaboration shortens the trust gap. Viewers are far more likely to watch and subscribe when a familiar creator is involved. Even small creators can benefit here; working with someone slightly ahead of you can introduce your channel to viewers who are already primed to care about your niche.

Collaboration isn't about size. It's about overlap, generosity, and shared value. Some of the fastest-growing channels grow through relationships, not virality.

Beginner-Friendly Ways to Collaborate (Even With a Small Channel)

Collaborations don't require a massive following or a formal partnership. At its simplest, a collaboration is just two creators finding a way to help each other grow.

Some easy ways to start:

- **Guest appearances:** Invite another creator (or even a knowledgeable friend) to appear briefly in your video, share a quote, or answer a question on camera or via voiceover.
- **Shared content:** Create a video together, remotely or in person, on a topic you both care about. Each of you can upload your own version and point viewers to the other channel.
- **Shoutouts:** Mention or recommend another creator's video in your content and let them know you did. Many creators are happy to return the favor.
- **Skill swaps:** Offer something you're good at, editing, thumbnails, scripting, or feedback, in exchange for exposure, a quick shoutout, or collaborative content.

The key is **generosity**. Offer value first, build genuine relationships, and stay open to creative ways of supporting others. You're not building a channel in isolation. Some of your most meaningful growth will come from the partnerships and friendships you form along the way.

Speeding Up Your Growth: A Beginner's Guide to Paid Promotion

While **organic growth** (people finding you naturally) is the foundation of a healthy channel, sometimes you want to give a specific video an extra push. This is where **Paid Promotion** comes in. In 2026, YouTube has made this process incredibly simple for beginners through a tool called **YouTube Promote**.

Think of paid promotion as **buying a ticket** for your video to be seen by a specific group of people who aren't currently following you. It is a way to skip the line and get your content in front of a new audience immediately.

The Easy Way: YouTube Promote

For most beginners, the best way to start is the **Promotions** tab inside **YouTube Studio**. Unlike the complex world of **Google Ads**, this tool is designed for creators, not professional marketing agencies.

How to set it up:

1. **Go to YouTube Studio:** On your desktop, click on the **Content** tab.
2. **Find the Promotions Tab:** You'll see this at the top of the screen alongside **Videos, Shorts,** and **Live.**
3. **Click New Promotion:**
    - **Choose Your Video:** Select the video you want to push. I recommend picking your best-performing video, the one that already has good comments and likes!
    - **Set Your Goal:** Do you want more **subscribers,** more **views,** or more **website visits?**
    - **Pick Your Audience:** You can choose the countries and languages you want to target. In 2026, you can even select **interests** (like **Cooking, Gaming,** or **Travel**) to ensure your video is shown to people who actually care about your niche.
    - **Set Your Budget:** You can start with as little as **$5 or $10**. You set a **Total Budget** and an end date, so you never have to worry about being overcharged.

How Paid Ads Actually Look

When you use YouTube Promote, your video usually appears in two places:

- **In-Feed:** Your video thumbnail appears in search results or on the **Watch Next** list with a small **"Sponsored"** label. If someone clicks it, they go straight to your video.
- **Shorts Feed:** If you promote a Short, it appears between other Shorts as people scroll.

Three Golden Rules for Paid Promotion

Before you spend your first dollar, keep these tips in mind to ensure you get the most value for your money:

1. **Promote Your Winner:** Don't use ads to try and **save** a video that nobody is watching. Instead, find the video that your current fans love the most and use ads to show it to **more** people just like them.
2. **Check Your Organic Data First:** As we discussed in the previous chapter, use the **Organic filter** to make sure your video is actually holding people's attention naturally. If the video is boring, paying for views won't help you gain loyal subscribers.
3. **Watch Your Blended Stats:** Remember that when you run an ad, your overall channel averages might look a bit lower (since you are reaching **cold strangers**). Use the **Organic vs. Paid** filters in your Analytics to see how your channel is growing naturally while the ad is running.

Important Note: Views and subscribers gained through paid promotions **do not count** toward the 4,000 public watch hours needed for the **YouTube Partner Program** (Monetization). Think of ads as a way to build your brand and community, not a shortcut to getting paid by YouTube.

Promotion Helps the Algorithm Too

Promotion isn't just for humans; it feeds YouTube's systems. In the first twenty-four to forty-eight hours after publishing, YouTube looks closely at how people respond. Are they clicking? Are they watching past the opening? Are they engaging? When you share your video and bring in even a small wave of real viewers, you're giving YouTube the signals it needs to decide whether your video deserves wider distribution. You don't need thousands of views. Sometimes ten or twenty intentional viewers are enough to get the flywheel moving.

Your Action Steps for Today

1. Choose one promotion channel. Pick a single platform that feels natural to you and share your latest video in a way that fits that space. This could be a short teaser clip, a thoughtful post explaining who the video is for, or a casual mention inside a relevant community.

2. Explore one collaboration opportunity. Identify one creator in your niche you genuinely respect and think about a simple way to work together. This could be a joint video, a shared Short, or using YouTube's collaboration feature.

3. Track where your views come from. Over the next few days, open **YouTube Studio → Analytics → Traffic sources** and observe where views are coming from. Notice which types of promotion bring in the most engagement and interest.

Optional Reflection

Which type of promotion felt easiest and most natural for you? Which felt forced? Growth is sustainable when it aligns with who you are, not when it feels like shouting into the void.

Tomorrow, we'll focus on **community building and** how to turn viewers into regulars and regulars into people who actually care about your channel and come back intentionally.

Day 24: Turning Viewers Into a Community

Up to this point, you've focused on setting up your channel, creating videos, and getting them in front of people. Now comes one of the most important shifts you'll make as a creator: **moving from simply attracting viewers to building a community.** A community on YouTube doesn't mean millions of subscribers or constant viral hits. It means creating a space where people feel welcome, recognized, and connected to what you're making. When someone comes back for a second video, leaves a comment, or subscribes, they're doing more than watching content. They're choosing you, and that choice is what turns a channel into something sustainable. Algorithms can help you get discovered, but community is what keeps people around. Viewers stay loyal to creators they feel connected to. These are creators who listen, respond, and show up consistently. Over time, that loyalty leads to better watch time, more engagement, organic sharing, and a much more fulfilling creative experience.

The Community Tab: Your Channel's Social Feed

Before we dive into engagement tactics, you need to know about your most powerful bridge: the **Community Tab**. In 2026, this isn't just an optional feature; it's a built-in social network for your channel. It allows you to stay visible in your subscribers' feeds between video uploads using text, images, and polls.

What is the Community Tab?

Think of it as your channel's **status update** area. It keeps your channel **alive** even when you aren't filming. For small channels, it is a massive growth engine because the algorithm pushes engaging community posts to **non-subscribers** who watch similar content. A single viral poll can often bring in more new viewers than a standard video.

- **How to Unlock It:** The tab typically unlocks once you reach **500 subscribers**. Once eligible, a new **Community** or **Posts** tab will appear on your channel page.
- **How to Post:** Hit the **Create (+)** icon on mobile or the camera icon in **YouTube Studio** and select **Create Post**.

You aren't limited to just text; you can mix and match different formats to see what resonates most with your unique audience.

- **Polls (The Engagement King):** These are the highest-performing posts for reach. You can create **Text Polls** (up to five options) or **Image Polls** (up to four images).
    - Use polls to let viewers vote on your next video topic or to share a **hot take** in your niche.
- **Quizzes:** Test your audience's knowledge with a multiple-choice question. You can even include an explanation that appears after they vote, making it a great tool for educational channels.
- **Image & Carousel Posts:** Share a single high-quality photo or a **carousel** of up to five images.
    - Use these for **Behind-the-Scenes** looks at your setup, **Day in the Life snapshots**, or even to share a **quick infographic.**
- **GIFs:** Animated images are perfect for showing your personality, sharing a reaction, or celebrating a channel milestone.
- **Video Links:** You can share your own latest upload or even a video from another creator you admire. This is a great way to **revive** older evergreen content from your back catalog.
- **Text-Only Updates:** Perfect for quick announcements, personal thoughts, or a simple **check-in** to see how your community is doing.

Pro-Tip: You can now set your community posts to automatically expire after twenty-four hours. This is perfect for **Flash Giveaways**, limited-time questions, or reminders for a live stream that's happening today. It creates a sense of have-to-be-there urgency for your most active fans.

What Engagement Really Means on YouTube

Engagement is any action a viewer takes beyond passively watching. This includes comments, likes, dislikes, shares, subscriptions, replies, and clicks on links, cards, or end screens. Each of these signals tells YouTube that your video is resonating with real people, and each one strengthens the relationship between you and your audience. But engagement isn't just about pleasing the algorithm. It's how conversations begin. It's how viewers go from being anonymous numbers to familiar names you recognize.

Encouraging Engagement Without Feeling Pushy

You don't need to beg for likes or interrupt your video with aggressive calls to action. Most engagement happens when viewers feel invited, not pressured. Asking a simple, specific question works far better than vague requests. Instead of "Let me know what you think," try something like, "What part of this was most helpful for you?" or "Have you tried this before?" Letting viewers know you read and reply to comments also makes a difference; it signals that their time and thoughts matter. **Pinned comments** are another powerful tool. You can use them to start a conversation, add context, or guide viewers to a related video. Over time, these small gestures shape how people experience your channel.

How to Pin a Comment

Whether you are on your phone or your computer, the process takes only a few seconds:

1. **Post Your Comment:** Type out your message in the comment section of your video and hit Comment. (You can also choose a great comment from a fan).
2. **Find the More Menu:** Hover over your comment (on desktop) or tap the **three vertical dots** (on mobile) to the right of the text.
3. **Select Pin:** Click on the **Pin** icon. A pop-up will ask you to confirm. Click on **Pin** again.
4. **Check for the Badge:** You will now see a small "Pinned by [Your Channel Name]" badge, and that comment will stay at the very top, even if the video gets thousands of other replies.

How to Add Maximum Value

Don't just say, "Thanks for watching!" Use this prime real estate to actively grow your channel:

- **The Ask-and-Pin Strategy:** Instead of a generic question, ask a **choice question**. **Example**: "Are you Team A or Team B? Let me know why below!" This lowers the **effort** for a viewer to reply, leading to a much busier comment section.

- **The Treasure Map (Timestamps):** If your video is long, pin a list of **Chapter timestamps**. This keeps viewers on the page longer as they **jump** to the parts they find most interesting, which signals high interest to YouTube.
- **The Bridge to More Content:** If you mention a tool or another video, put that link in the pinned comment. Viewers find it much faster than digging through the description.
- **The Retention Anchor:** While people are reading your interesting pinned comment, your video is still playing in the background. This subtly boosts your **watch time** and tells the algorithm that your content is holding people's attention.

By taking thirty seconds to pin a thoughtful comment, you are transforming a static video into an active community hub. It's a small gesture that makes your viewers feel invited to stay, speak up, and return for more.

Why Responding to Comments Builds Loyalty

Replying to comments may feel minor, but it's one of the strongest trust-building habits you can develop. When viewers feel seen, they're far more likely to return. In the beginning, when your videos have only a handful of comments, make it a habit to reply to every single one, especially within the first 24 hours after publishing. This is the best time to slow down, be thoughtful, and create real connections. Early viewers often become your most loyal supporters because they remember being acknowledged. You don't need to respond to every comment forever to make an impact. Engaging early helps create momentum and encourages more people to join the conversation. It can also help your video perform better, since active discussions signal relevance and interest to YouTube. A simple thank-you, a thoughtful reply, or a short follow-up question can turn a one-time viewer into a regular.

From Viewers to Subscribers to True Fans

Subscriber count matters far less than subscriber quality. A smaller group of active, engaged subscribers will outperform a large, silent audience every time. Consistency plays a big role here. When people know what kind of content you make and when to expect it, subscribing feels like a natural choice. Clear themes, familiar formats, and gentle reminders to subscribe help viewers understand why staying connected is worthwhile. Over time, inviting your audience behind the scenes, sharing what you're working on next, asking for feedback, or explaining your thought process helps transform subscribers into supporters who feel invested in your journey.

Building a Brand vs. Just Getting Views

In 2026, it is easier than ever to get a **hit** video, but harder than ever to build a brand. High views are just a metric; a **brand** is an emotional response. It's the consistency, values, and trust that make a viewer recognize your work instantly.

To build a lasting brand, you have to look beyond the view count and focus on the **quality** of the attention you are getting. Top creators categorize views into three distinct types:

1. **Forgettable Views:** The viewer watches, gets a quick answer or a laugh, and forgets you existed five seconds later. These help your reach, but they don't build a community.
2. **Regrettable Views:** This is the **clickbait trap.** The viewer feels tricked or like they wasted their time. This builds a **negative** brand, making it harder for them to ever trust your thumbnail again.
3. **Memorable Views:** These are the views that stick. The viewer leaves the video thinking differently about a topic or feeling a genuine connection to you.

The Goal: Creating "Memorable Minutes"

Shift your goal from chasing a massive view count to creating **Memorable Minutes**. If you can provide ten minutes of high-value, high-trust content to 1,000 people, you have a much stronger brand than someone who gets **100,000 forgettable clicks**. Memorable minutes are what turn a casual viewer into a lifelong fan.

Using Live Streams to Deepen Connection

Live streaming is one of the most direct ways to build those **memorable minutes** in real-time. It allows real-time interaction, questions, and conversation, something prerecorded videos can't fully replicate. In 2026, YouTube has made live streaming far more accessible and creator-friendly. One of the biggest improvements is **Practice Before Live**, a mode designed to let you rehearse without pressure, especially useful for vertical live streams. Here's **how to use Practice Before Live step by step**:

1. First, open **YouTube Studio** on desktop or mobile and click on **Create (+) → Go Live**.
2. Choose **Vertical Live** or a standard live stream, depending on your format.
3. Before you go live, you'll see an option labeled **Practice Before Live**. Select this mode instead of going public. This opens a private rehearsal session that only you can see.
4. During practice mode, you can test everything exactly as if you were live:
    - Check your camera framing and lighting.
    - Test your microphone and audio levels.
    - Practice your opening, pacing, and transitions.
    - Make sure your internet connection is stable.
5. Nothing is shown to viewers, and no notifications are sent. This gives you a calm, pressure-free space to get comfortable.
6. When you're ready, you don't need to restart. Simply click on **Go Live** (or **Transition to Public**) from within the practice session. Your stream will instantly become public, and subscribers will be notified.

This workflow removes one of the biggest barriers to live streaming: fear of messing up at the start. You get to warm up, settle in, and begin confidently, without technical surprises or awkward first minutes. For beginners, this means you can treat live streaming like any other skill: rehearse first, then perform. If you have **channel memberships enabled** (discussed in the next chapter), there's also a new option to start a live stream as public and then transition it to members-only mid-stream. This allows you to welcome everyone initially and then reward your most loyal supporters with exclusive access, creating a stronger sense of belonging. YouTube has also introduced **AI-powered live stream highlights**, which automatically identify engaging moments from your live streams and turn them into Shorts. This means your live content doesn't disappear once the stream ends; it can continue reaching new viewers through the Shorts feed and act as an entry point into your community.

Key Ideas to Keep in Mind

You don't need scale to build connection. A small, engaged audience is enough to create momentum. People may discover you for your content, but they stay for how you make them feel. Engagement works best when it's mutual, when you show up for your viewers as much as you want them to show up for you. At its core, YouTube is not just a publishing platform. It's a conversation.

Your Action Steps for Today

1. Engage with your audience directly. Go to the comments on your most recent video and respond to what's there. Thank someone for watching, answer a question, or acknowledge their support. The goal is to show that there's a real person behind the channel.

2. Create the first conversation if needed. If your video doesn't have comments yet, take initiative. Leave a thoughtful comment on a creator you genuinely enjoy, then return to your own video and add a pinned comment that invites discussion. A simple question is enough to open the door.

3. Brainstorm about live connection. Spend a few minutes considering how live content could fit into your channel. You don't need to go live yet; just imagine whether a short live session, Q&A, or practice stream might help you connect more deeply with viewers in the future.

Optional Reflection

What kind of community do you want to build around your channel? Write down two or three small ways you can make your content feel more human, welcoming, and interactive over the next month.

Tomorrow, we'll look at how creators turn **engaged audiences into income** and explore **AdSense**, sponsorships, and long-term monetization paths that support sustainable growth.

Day 25: Monetization Models That Scale (Ads, Brands, Products)

By this point in the journey, you've learned how to create content, grow visibility, and build real connections with viewers. Today's focus is on turning that effort into income in a way that's realistic, ethical, and sustainable.

Monetization on YouTube in 2026 isn't about chasing one magic source of money; it's about layering multiple income streams that grow alongside your channel. The most successful creators don't rely on virality. They rely on systems.

This chapter will help you understand the monetization models available to you, how they work together, and how to choose the ones that actually fit your content and audience.

The Two Lanes of YouTube Income

In 2026, the simplest way to think about your earnings is to divide them into **two lanes**. One lane is what YouTube pays you for being a creator on their platform, and the other is what you earn yourself by using YouTube as a megaphone for your own business.

The **first is platform-based monetization**. This is the **automatic** income that comes through the **YPP**. Once you meet the eligibility requirements (like 500 or 1,000 subscribers), YouTube handles the billing and pays you directly. These include ad revenue, YouTube Premium revenue, memberships, Super Thanks, and shopping integrations.

The **second is creator-driven monetization,** which includes sponsorships, affiliate marketing, products, services, and anything you build independently of YouTube's payouts. You aren't waiting for a **payout** from YouTube; instead, you are working directly with brands or your own customers.

The real power comes when these two lanes support each other. Platform income rewards consistency and watch time. Creator-driven income rewards trust, relevance, and clarity. Together, they create stability.

AdSense: The Baseline, Not the End Goal

AdSense is usually the first monetization milestone creators think about, and for good reason. Once you're accepted into the **YPP**, you can earn a share of revenue from ads shown on your videos. This includes skippable ads, non-skippable ads, display ads on desktop, sponsored cards, and mid-roll ads on videos longer than eight minutes.

The reason two channels with the same number of views can have wildly different paychecks comes down to three main factors: **niche, location, and content type.**

- **Your Niche (Topic):** Advertisers pay more to reach people who are about to make a major purchase. In 2026, niches like **personal finance, business, and AI tools** often see the highest rates because the **buying power** of that audience is high. In contrast, general entertainment or gaming might have lower rates but can make up for it with a much larger number of views.
- **Audience Location:** Advertisers in countries like the **US, UK, Canada, and Australia** generally have larger marketing budgets. A view from one of these regions often pays significantly more than a view from a region where the local currency or advertiser demand is lower.
- **Content Type and Length:** Videos over **eight minutes** long are a creator's best friend because they allow for **mid-roll ads**, extra ad breaks in the middle of the video. Additionally, evergreen content (like tutorials) tends to earn more over time than trending content because it stays relevant and searchable for years.

As we've discussed, you don't need to be an accountant to understand your earnings, but you should keep these two **beginner-friendly** definitions in mind:

- **CPM (Cost Per Mille):** This is the **Sticker Price**. It is what **advertisers pay** to show ads to 1,000 people. It reflects how much the market values your audience.
- **RPM (Revenue Per Mille):** This is your **take-home pay.** It is what you actually earn per 1,000 views after YouTube takes its 45% cut. RPM is the most important number for you because it includes all your earnings, including ads and YouTube Premium.

It's a mistake to wait for a **viral hit** to make you rich. **AdSense** is designed to reward **scale and consistency.** A viral video might give you a one-time spike, but a channel that builds a reliable library of content will earn a growing, predictable paycheck month after month.

Think of **AdSense** as your **base salary**. It covers your expenses and gear upgrades, giving you the freedom to explore even higher-paying opportunities like brand deals and digital products. Payments are issued monthly once your **AdSense** balance reaches the payout threshold, and income must be reported for tax purposes depending on your country.

Fan-Funded Monetization: Letting Viewers Support You Directly

In 2026, fan-supported tools have become one of the most meaningful ways for creators, especially smaller or niche channels, to earn income without relying solely on ads. These features allow viewers to support you because they value your work, your voice, and the community you're building, not because an ad happened to play before a video.

Fan funding works best when trust already exists. You don't need a huge audience to make it effective. A small group of engaged viewers who genuinely appreciate your content can often contribute more, emotionally and financially, than a large but passive audience. This kind of monetization turns appreciation into sustainability and gives your most loyal viewers a way to actively participate in your journey. Here's how each fan-funded feature works and how you can use them thoughtfully.

Channel Memberships: Building Your Inner Circle

Think of channel memberships as a **VIP pass** to your content. In 2026, this feature has evolved into a powerful way to create a recurring income stream while rewarding your most dedicated fans with a closer look at your process.

How to Set the Stage

Memberships are best introduced once you have a clear content direction and a small but vocal group of fans who regularly comment on your videos. To start, you'll need to be part of the **YPP**. Once you hit the eligibility requirements (500 or 1,000 subscribers depending on your path), you can navigate to the **Earn** tab in YouTube Studio to begin the setup.

Designing Your Tiers

Tier	Purpose	Recommended Price	Key Perk Ideas
Starter	Casual Support	$1.99 - $2.99	Loyalty badges, custom emojis, and members-only community polls.
Core Fan	The Inner Circle	$4.99 - $9.99	Everything above + early access to videos and monthly shoutouts.
Super Supporter	High Value	$14.99 - $24.99	Everything above + exclusive behind-the-scenes vlogs or monthly Q&As.

In 2026, the most successful beginner strategy is to offer **two to three clear pricing tiers**. You want to make it easy for casual supporters to join while giving **superfans** a way to truly invest in you.

Pro-Tips for Managing Perks

The biggest mistake beginners make is offering perks that take too much time to create, leading to burnout. Focus on **high-value, low-effort** rewards:

- **Early Access:** Simply schedule your public videos to go live for members twenty-four to forty-eight hours early. It costs you $0 and zero extra minutes but makes members feel like VIPs.
- **Polls & Decisions:** Give members a **vote** on your next video topic or thumbnail choice via the **Community Tab.** This builds deep loyalty because they feel like co-creators.
- **Exclusive Emojis:** Design three to five **inside joke emojis** that members can use in your comments. It builds a shared language that only your **inner circle** understands.

One Final Tip: Always keep it simple. It's better to offer two perks you can deliver perfectly every time than five perks that you struggle to keep up with.

Super Thanks: The Virtual Tip Jar

Super Thanks is one of the most accessible fan-funding tools on YouTube because it doesn't require you to be **live**. It allows your viewers to show extra appreciation for any of your regular videos or Shorts at any time.

- **How it Works:** When a viewer clicks the **Thanks button** (a heart with a dollar sign), they can choose a one-time tip amount. In exchange, they get a colorful, one-time animation over the video and a distinct, highlighted comment in your comment section.
- **The Strategy:** You don't need an elaborate sales pitch. Often, a simple, human reminder at the end of your video, like "If this guide helped you, feel free to use the Super Thanks button to support the channel," is enough to nudge your most grateful viewers.
- **Engagement Tip:** You can now **reply to a Super Thanks comment with a Short**. This is a powerful 2026 feature that lets you publicly thank a supporter with a personalized video clip, making them feel like a true part of your journey.

Super Chats and Super Stickers: Boosting Live Interaction

While Super Thanks is for uploaded content, **Super Chats** and **Super Stickers** are designed specifically for the high-energy environment of live streams.

- **Super Chats:** Viewers pay to have their message highlighted and pinned to the top of the live chat. The more they spend, the longer their message stays pinned (up to five hours for the highest tier). This is perfect for Q&As, as it helps you identify the questions your fans are most eager to have answered.
- **Super Stickers:** These are fun, animated graphics that viewers can purchase to pop up in the chat. They are great for **hype** moments, like when you reach a milestone or finish a difficult tutorial live on air.
- **The Best Approach:** These features thrive on **real-time recognition**. When a Super Chat comes in, try to acknowledge it verbally: "Hey, thanks so much to [Name] for the Super Chat! That's a great question; let's dive into it." This immediate feedback

encourages others to participate and makes your live sessions feel more like a community hangout than a one-way broadcast.

The Payout: For all Supers (Thanks, Chats, and Stickers), you generally keep **70% of the revenue** after YouTube's 30% cut. It's a transparent way to see exactly how your community is helping you build your creative business.

What makes these tools powerful is not the money alone: it's the relationship they reinforce. When someone chooses to support you directly, they're saying, "This content matters to me." Acknowledging that support, by thanking supporters verbally, replying to highlighted comments, or offering small moments of recognition, goes a long way in strengthening community loyalty. Fan-funded monetization isn't about asking constantly or putting pressure on viewers. It's about creating content worth supporting and making it easy for people who want to give back to do so. When used with honesty and restraint, these tools can become a steady, confidence-boosting income stream that grows naturally alongside your channel.

Sponsorships: Where Trust Turns Into Income

Brand partnerships are one of the highest-earning paths for many creators, and they don't require millions of subscribers. Brands care about relevance, audience alignment, and credibility far more than raw size.

Sponsorships can range from a short mention to a full dedicated video. The most effective ones feel natural: products you already use, tools that genuinely help your audience, or services that fit seamlessly into your content. If you want to attract sponsors, consistency matters. So does clarity. Make it obvious what your channel is about and who it's for. Add a business inquiry email to your channel, and don't be afraid to reach out to smaller brands you already trust. Many creators land their first deals by initiating the conversation.

Affiliate Marketing: Earning Through Recommendations

Affiliate income is one of the most accessible monetization models for creators at any stage. When you recommend a product or service using a tracked link, you earn a commission if someone makes a purchase. This model works particularly well for tutorials, reviews, and educational content. The key is transparency and alignment. Only promote products you actually believe in, and always disclose affiliate relationships clearly. Long-term trust is worth far more than short-term clicks.

YouTube Shopping Affiliate Program (2026 Update)

In 2026, YouTube's Shopping affiliate program has become a major monetization option for eligible creators, especially those who create product-focused or recommendation-based content.

At its core, this program uses **affiliate marketing**, which simply means **earning a small commission when someone buys a product through your recommendation**. You don't create or ship the product, and the buyer doesn't pay extra. Instead, the brand or retailer pays you for helping drive the sale.

This program allows you to tag products directly in your videos and live streams. Viewers can see pricing and product details without leaving YouTube, then complete their purchase on the retailer's site. You earn a commission when a purchase is made, and everything, from tagging to earnings, is managed inside YouTube Studio.

However, you don't have to be eligible for the **YouTube Shopping Affiliate Program,** you can also start earning on your very first video using standard affiliate links. Normal affiliate links work as follows:

- **Amazon Associates:** This is still the gold standard for beginners. You don't need a large following to sign up. You simply create a link for a product you love and place it in your description. Head to www.affiliate-program.amazon.com to sign up.
- **The Anything-Else Bonus:** One of the best-kept secrets of affiliate marketing is that you often earn a commission even if the viewer doesn't buy the exact product you linked. If they click your Amazon link for a $10 book but end up buying a $500 coffee machine during that same session, **you still get a cut of the total sale.**
- **Trust is the Currency:** Never promote things you don't like for a quick buck. In 2026, viewers are savvy; if they feel you're just a salesperson, they won't return. Only link products you genuinely use or recommend.

While Amazon Associates is the most popular way to start on Day One, YouTube has built its **own pro version** of this system. If you aren't interested in managing multiple external accounts and want a more integrated experience, you can switch to **YouTube's Shopping Affiliate Program** once you qualify. Here is what it entails:

- **Clickable Tagging:** Instead of telling people to **check the link in the description**, you can **tag** a product so a small shopping bag icon appears right on the screen. Viewers can click on it to see the price and details without ever stopping the video.
- **One-Stop Paycheck:** You don't have to log into ten different websites to check your sales. Whether you recommend a product from Target, Walmart, or Sephora, all your commissions are grouped together and paid through your main **YouTube AdSense account.**
- **Easier for the Viewer:** Because the experience is so smooth, people are much more likely to buy. It feels less like a **sales pitch** and more like a helpful feature of the video.

The Strategy: Start with Amazon or direct brand links in your description today. Use them to build your affiliate muscle. Then, once you hit eligibility criteria, transition to the **YouTube Shopping Affiliate Program** for your most popular products to maximize your earnings.

Eligibility for the Affiliate Program

To join the **YouTube Shopping Affiliate Program** and earn commissions by tagging products from other brands, your channel must meet these specific requirements:

- **10,000 Subscribers:** This program currently requires a larger audience than the standard monetization tiers.
- **Member of YPP:** You must already be part of the **YouTube Partner Program.**
- **Location:** You must be based in an eligible country (such as the US, UK, Brazil, India, Korea, and several others).
- **Channel Type:** Your channel cannot be set as **Made for Kids** or be an Official Artist Channel.

How to Check Eligibility in YouTube Studio

1. Sign in to **YouTube Studio**.
2. Navigate to the **Earn tab.**
3. **Look for Shopping:** Scroll down to the **Programs** or **Ways to Earn** section.
4. **View Status:** If your location is eligible, you will see a card for the **YouTube Shopping Affiliate Program** with a **Get Started** or **Join Now** button. If your country is not yet supported, this option will be hidden, or you will see a message stating that the feature is unavailable in your region.

How to Tag Products

Once you have enabled **Shopping** in the **Earn** tab of YouTube Studio, tagging products is a seamless part of your upload workflow. You can tag up to **thirty products** in a single video or live stream.

For New Videos and Shorts (Mobile)

1. **Upload Your Video:** Start the upload process in the YouTube app.
2. **Tap Tag Products:** On the final details screen, look for the **Tag Products** option.
3. **Search and Select:** Type the name of the product you are featuring. YouTube will show you a list of approved retailers (like Amazon, Walmart, or Target).
4. **Place the Sticker (Shorts Only):** For Shorts, you can choose exactly where the **Shopping** sticker appears on the screen so it doesn't cover important visuals.

For Existing Content (Desktop)

1. **Go to YouTube Studio:** Navigate to the **Content** tab.
2. **Select a Video:** Click on the video you want to edit.
3. **Click on Products:** In the right-hand menu, click the **Products** box.

4. **Add Timestamps:** This is a key 2026 feature. You can now tag a product to appear at a **specific time** in your video. For example, if you talk about a camera at 02:45, you can make the product tag pop up exactly then.

For Live Streams

1. **Plan Ahead:** In the **Live Control Room**, click the **Shopping** tab.
2. **Select Your Lineup:** Search and add the products you plan to show during the stream.
3. **Pin Your Star:** During the live broadcast, you can **pin** a specific product to the top of the chat. This is perfect for when you are doing a deep-dive review of one specific item.

This system reduces friction, improves viewer experience, and turns content into a direct shopping pathway, especially powerful during live streams, tutorials, and reviews.

Products, Services, and Ownership-Based Income

Beyond **ads** and **affiliate marketing**, many creators build income streams they fully own. Digital products like templates, ebooks, and courses can generate passive income once created. Print-on-demand merchandise allows you to sell without managing inventory. Coaching, consulting, and freelance services let your content act as a client funnel.

These options take more upfront effort but offer the highest level of control and scalability. Over time, they often become the most stable part of a creator's income.

Realistic Expectations and Long-Term Thinking

Most creators don't earn meaningful income right away. Monetization builds gradually, alongside skills, content quality, and audience trust. Early earnings may be inconsistent or small, and that's normal.

Every video you publish is an asset. Over time, your library compounds. Monetization becomes less about individual uploads and more about systems working together. The goal isn't quick money. It's sustainable growth that supports both your creativity and your life.

Your Action Steps for Today

1. Check your monetization readiness. Open **YouTube Studio** and review your monetization status. Make sure your **AdSense** account is set up and connected, even if you're not eligible for monetization yet. This removes friction later when you hit the requirements.

2. Identify aligned income paths. Brainstorm one or two monetization options that feel natural for your content and audience. This might be ads, affiliate links, digital products, or services you could offer in the future.

3. Explore what's coming next. If available, visit the **Earn** tab in YouTube Studio to see which monetization features you'll unlock as your channel grows. Familiarity now makes activation easier later.

Optional Reflection

What kind of income would feel both sustainable and motivating for you? Clarifying this early will help you make smarter, less reactive decisions as your channel develops.

Tomorrow, we'll shift focus to treating your **channel like a real business** and organizing income, planning for taxes, and building systems that support long-term success without burnout.

Day 26: Managing Income, Expenses, and Creator Finances

Once money starts coming in from YouTube, even a small amount, it changes how your channel functions. What begins as a creative project slowly becomes something closer to a business. That doesn't mean spreadsheets all day or hiring an accountant tomorrow. It simply means building habits now that will protect your time, your money, and your peace of mind later. Many creators wait too long to get organized and end up scrambling during tax season or losing track of where their income actually comes from. This chapter is about avoiding that stress by putting a simple system in place early: one that grows with you.

Why Financial Organization Matters for Creators

Financial organization isn't about being corporate. It's about clarity. Once you earn money on YouTube, you're responsible for reporting it correctly, understanding where it comes from, and knowing where it goes. In many countries, including the U.S., earning above certain thresholds triggers tax reporting requirements. For example, **AdSense** income may result in tax forms being issued once you pass an annual earning threshold of $2,000. Not receiving a form doesn't mean the income doesn't count. Any money you earn is still your responsibility to report. Beyond taxes, organization helps you track payout thresholds, manage income that comes from multiple sources, and understand whether your channel is actually profitable. It also makes it easier to claim legitimate expenses, which can reduce how much you owe at the end of the year depending on local tax laws.

What to Track (Even at the Beginning)

You don't need advanced software to stay organized. What matters is consistency. At a minimum, start tracking two things: what comes in and what goes out. On the income side, this includes **AdSense payouts**, **brand deals** or **sponsorship payments**, **affiliate commissions**, fan-supported income like **Super Thanks or memberships**, and any sales from digital products or merchandise.

On the expense side, track anything you purchase specifically for your channel. This may include cameras, microphones, lighting, editing software, design tools, online courses, website hosting, or promotional services. Keep receipts whenever possible; even screenshots or emailed confirmations are enough to start. You'll also want a place to store important documents such as tax forms, invoices, contracts, and payment confirmations. A simple folder structure, digital or physical, goes a long way. A basic spreadsheet in Google Sheets or Excel is more than enough in the beginning. List each transaction by date, category, amount, and source. If you prefer tools, platforms like Notion or free bookkeeping apps can help, but simplicity beats complexity every time.

Separating Personal and Channel Finances

As soon as you begin earning, separating your creator finances from your personal spending becomes one of the smartest moves you can make. This doesn't require registering a company right away. Often, opening a separate checking account just for YouTube-related income and expenses is enough. Using a dedicated card for gear, subscriptions, or software helps keep records clean and prevents confusion later. Even a monthly habit of reviewing what came in and what went out builds awareness. You start seeing patterns: which income streams are growing, which expenses are recurring, and whether your channel is moving toward sustainability. This separation also makes tax preparation dramatically easier.

Do You Need to Register as a Business?

For most beginners, the answer is no, at least not yet. Many creators operate as individuals or sole owners in the early stages. That's completely normal. Formal business registration usually becomes relevant when income is consistent, when you're signing contracts regularly, when you want clearer legal separation, or when you plan to hire help. The rules vary by country, so it's worth checking local guidelines or speaking to a tax professional once money becomes meaningful. The important thing now is awareness, not paperwork.

Understanding U.S. Tax Requirements for YouTube Earnings (Even If You're Not in the U.S.)

One of the most confusing parts of earning on YouTube is taxes, especially because **U.S. tax rules apply to all monetized creators worldwide**, not just creators living in the U.S. If you are part of the **YPP**, Google is legally required to collect tax information from you and, in some cases, withhold taxes on your behalf. This applies whether you live in the U.S., Europe, Asia, or anywhere else. The most important thing to know as a beginner is this: **submitting your tax information is not optional**. If you don't do it, Google may automatically withhold a large percentage of your earnings.

Why Google Collects U.S. Tax Information

Under U.S. tax law, Google must report and, when required, withhold taxes on **YouTube earnings generated from viewers in the U.S.** This includes income from:

- Ads (**AdSense**).
- Super Chats, Super Stickers, and Super Thanks.
- Channel Memberships.

Google does this under rules set by the U.S. Internal Revenue Service (IRS). YouTube and Google are not allowed to give tax advice; they are simply required to enforce these rules.

What Happens If You Don't Submit Tax Info

If you don't submit valid tax information in **AdSense for YouTube**, Google may be required to withhold taxes at the **maximum rate**, which can be very costly:

- **Individual accounts:** up to **24% of total earnings worldwide.**
- **Business accounts:** up to **30% of U.S. earnings**, and in some cases **24% worldwide.**

This withholding continues **until valid tax information is submitted**, even if you don't live in the U.S. or haven't earned much yet. Submitting your tax information early protects you from unnecessary deductions later.

Tax Treaties (Why They Matter a Lot)

If you live outside the U.S., you might notice that Google is required to withhold taxes from the money you earn from **U.S.-based viewers**. However, depending on where you live, you may be able to significantly reduce this tax through a **tax treaty.** A tax treaty is essentially an agreement between your country and the U.S. to ensure you aren't taxed twice on the same income.

How It Works

- **The Default Rate:** Without a tax treaty, Google may be required to withhold up to **30%** of your earnings from U.S. viewers.
- **The Treaty Rate:** If your country has a treaty, this rate can drop to **15%, 10%, or even 0%**.
- **The Catch:** Google will **not** apply this discount automatically. You must explicitly claim the treaty benefits when you fill out your tax information in **AdSense**.

How to Claim Your Benefits

When you reach the **Tax Treaty** section of your **AdSense** tax form:

1. **Select Yes:** When asked if you are claiming a reduced rate of withholding under a tax treaty.
2. **Select Your Country:** Choose your country of residence from the dropdown menu.
3. **Check the Boxes:** You will need to select the specific **Articles** and **Paragraphs** for the types of income you receive (such as **AdSense** and YouTube royalties). **AdSense** provides helpful tooltips to guide you through this.
4. **Provide Your TIN:** You will usually need to provide your local **Taxpayer Identification Number,** like your National

Insurance number, Permanent Account Number (PAN), or Unique Taxpayer Reference (UTR) to prove your residency.

Why This Matters

If you earn $1,000 from U.S. viewers, a 30% withholding means you only see $700. With a treaty that reduces the rate to 0%, you keep the full $1,000. It only takes a few minutes to fill out the form, but it can save you thousands of dollars as your channel grows. (**Note:** Tax laws can be complex. If you are unsure about your country's specific treaty or which tax ID to use, it is always a good idea to consult a local tax professional).

How Often You Need to Submit Tax Information

Even if nothing changes, **tax forms expire**. You must:

- Submit tax information when you first monetize.
- Re-submit it **every few years** (typically every three years).
- Update it anytime your legal address or status changes.

Creators are required to have valid tax information on file by **December 10th of each year**. Missing this deadline can trigger automatic withholding.

How to Submit or Update Your Tax Information (Step by Step)

1. Sign in to your **AdSense for YouTube** account.
2. Go to **Payments → Payments info.**
3. Click on **Manage settings.**
4. Find **U.S. tax info** and click on **Edit.**
5. Select **Manage tax info.**
6. Follow the guided form to choose the correct tax form for your situation.
7. Review, submit, and confirm that your status shows **Approved (green).**

After submission, you can view:

- Your withholding rate.
- Whether treaty benefits are applied.
- Any future updates needed.

What Gets Taxed (And What Doesn't)

Only the portion of your earnings **generated from U.S. viewers** is subject to U.S. withholding if you've submitted tax information. However, if you **don't submit tax information**, Google may withhold taxes on **your entire worldwide earnings**, not just U.S. income.

That's why submitting forms early is critical, even if most of your audience is outside the U.S.

A Simple Example (Beginner-Friendly)

Imagine you earn **$1,000** in a month.

- $900 comes from non-U.S. viewers.
- $100 comes from U.S. viewers.

Possible outcomes:

- **No tax information submitted:** Up to $240 withheld (24% of your total $1,000 worldwide earnings).
    - **Note:** Because you haven't proved where you live, YouTube must assume the highest **backup withholding rate** on every dollar you earned.
- **Tax information submitted + treaty claimed:** $15 withheld (15% of the $100 earned from U.S. viewers).
    - **Note:** By submitting your forms, you protect your $900 in non-U.S. earnings. The 15% rate is a special **discount** provided by the tax treaty between your country and the U.S.
- **Tax information submitted, no treaty:** $30 withheld (30% of the $100 earned from U.S. viewers).
    - **Note:** You still protected your $900 in non-U.S. earnings, but because your country doesn't have a treaty, you pay the standard 30% rate on U.S.-sourced income.

The content can be exactly the same. The difference comes down to how the paperwork is handled.

One Important Reminder

Google will **never** ask for your password or personal details by email. Only submit your tax information through your official **AdSense** account, and always verify that emails come from @youtube.com or @google.com.

Building a System That Grows With You

The best financial system is one you'll actually use. Start small. Track monthly income. Save receipts. Review numbers occasionally without judgment. As your channel grows, you can upgrade tools, add automation, or get professional advice. This may seem like a lot right now, but what matters is that you're treating your creative work with respect. Organization isn't restrictive; it's what gives you freedom to grow without chaos.

Your Action Steps for Today

1. **Set up a basic tracking system.** Create a simple spreadsheet or choose a free tool to track income and expenses related to your channel.

2. **Organize your documents.** Set up folders for receipts, contracts, payout confirmations, and tax-related documents, digital or physical.

3. **Log what you already have.** If you've earned money or spent money on your channel already, record those first entries so nothing is lost.

Optional Step

If you're ready, consider opening a separate bank account for your YouTube income and expenses.

Tomorrow, we'll zoom out and look at the **reality of a creator's workflow** and how YouTubers balance filming, editing, planning, and life without burning out.

Day 27: What Consistency Really Means in 2026

By now, you've probably realized something that surprises a lot of new creators: YouTube isn't just about filming videos. It's about managing energy, time, and expectations in a way that lets you keep going long after the excitement of your first uploads fades. Consistency doesn't mean posting every day or following a rigid schedule that burns you out. It means building a rhythm you can realistically maintain alongside the rest of your life. The creators who last aren't the ones who work the hardest for one month; they're the ones who find a pace they can return to again and again. To understand what that really looks like, it helps to zoom in on the day-to-day reality of running a channel.

A Realistic Look at a Creator's Workday

There's no single **correct YouTuber schedule**. Some creators upload weekly, others biweekly or monthly. Some work full-time jobs or study, while others dedicate more hours to content creation. Still, most creators move through the same core stages, just spread out differently. A typical production-focused day might begin with planning. This could mean refining a video outline, reviewing notes, checking title ideas, or making sure your main points are clear before you ever touch the camera.

Planning is quiet work, but it saves hours later. Filming usually comes next. This includes setting up your space, adjusting lighting and audio, recording your main footage, and occasionally redoing sections that don't land quite right. Many creators discover that filming takes less time than they expect but more mental energy. Editing often takes the longest. Cutting footage, removing pauses, adding captions or music, and reviewing the final export can stretch across one or several sessions. This is where pacing, clarity, and watchability really come together. Uploading and optimizing is its own phase. Writing descriptions, choosing thumbnails, adding end screens, scheduling the video, and double-checking settings all matter. This is also when many creators second-guess themselves, but it's part of the process. Finally, there's engagement and review. Sharing the video, responding to early comments, and glancing at initial analytics helps you close the loop and learn for next time. Some creators do all of this in one long day. Others spread it across a week. Both approaches are valid.

What Consistency Actually Looks Like Behind the Scenes

What viewers see is the final video. What they don't see is everything around it: troubleshooting tech issues, wrestling with self-doubt, rewriting intros, losing files, or wondering whether a video is **good enough**. Consistency isn't about avoiding these moments. It's about continuing despite them. In 2026, sustainable creators think in systems, not willpower. They reuse setups, repeat formats, and simplify decisions. They don't ask, "Can I do this perfectly?" They ask, "Can I do this again next week?" That mindset shift is what turns content creation from a stressful sprint into a manageable routine.

The Invisible Labor: Managing the Emotional Game

Consistency isn't just about showing up with a camera; it's about managing the internal friction that comes with it. It is important to recognize that the **work** of YouTube includes a heavy emotional load that a calendar or a checklist can't always solve.

- **Performance Pressure & Ego:** It is natural to feel your self-worth rise and fall with your view count. Learning to detach your identity from your **Day 1 analytics** is a skill you must practice. If a video performs poorly, it isn't a reflection of your value or your talent; it's simply a data point to help you adjust the next one.
- **The Hard Out and the Non-Upload:** Sometimes, a project just doesn't come together. Maybe the footage feels flat, the audio is distracting, or your energy on camera felt forced and insincere. Part of being a professional is having the courage to **not upload** content that doesn't meet your standards or protect your creative integrity. Consistency means staying in the game for the long haul, but it doesn't mean publishing work that you don't believe in.
- **The Social Dynamic:** Whether you are filming with a friend, interviewing an expert, or simply featuring family in a vlog, managing **on-camera chemistry** is an art. It requires setting clear boundaries and understanding that a great personal relationship doesn't always translate into a great on-screen collaboration, and that's okay. Protecting your real-world connections is always more important than any single upload.

Because these emotional hurdles are a natural part of the job, the best way to manage them is to build a structure that takes the pressure off your decision-making.

Designing a Rhythm That Fits Your Life

You don't need a strict timetable, but some structure helps. Many creators start by loosely assigning phases to different days: planning on one day, filming on another, editing in short sessions, and uploading when ready. Others batch several videos at once and then take breaks from filming entirely. What matters most is alignment. Your upload pace should match your available time, your energy levels, and your current season of life. Posting once a month consistently is far more powerful than posting weekly for a month and disappearing. Consistency is a promise you make to yourself first.

You Don't Need to Go Full-Time to Be Legit

One of the biggest myths about YouTube is that success requires all-in, full-time commitment. In reality, many successful channels are built slowly: around jobs, studies, caregiving, or other responsibilities. Consistency isn't measured in hours worked per day. It's measured by whether you keep showing up, learning, and improving over time. A creator who uploads thoughtfully and regularly, even at a slower pace, often outlasts someone chasing intensity. It's perfectly natural for your pace to shift over time. Growth rarely follows a straight line, much like the unpredictable rhythm of life itself.

Sample Timetable 1: A One-Day YouTube Workflow

This works well if you prefer to focus deeply and get everything done in one focused day.

Morning: Start with planning while your energy is fresh. Review your outline, clarify your main points, and double-check what the video is actually about. This is also a good time to quickly review your title idea so your filming stays focused.

Late Morning to Early Afternoon: Set up your filming space and record your video. Film your main talking footage first, then capture any extra shots you might need, like screen recordings or close-ups. Don't aim for perfection. Clarity is enough.

Mid Afternoon: Take a break. Stepping away helps you reset mentally and makes editing easier later.

Afternoon to Early Evening: Edit the video. Trim pauses, clean up audio, add captions or simple text, and export the final version. Watch it once through without overthinking it.

Evening: Upload and optimize. Add your title, description, thumbnail, and end screens. Schedule or publish the video, then respond to early comments if any come in.

This approach is intense but efficient, and many creators use it once or twice a month.

Sample Timetable 2: A Weekly YouTube Rhythm

This works better if you're balancing YouTube with work, school, or family and want less daily pressure.

Day 1: Planning. Brainstorm ideas, outline one video, and clarify your hook and key points. This usually takes less time than people expect.

Day 2: Filming. Set up once and record. If possible, film more than one video while everything is ready.

Day 3: Editing (Part 1). Do rough cuts: trimming, cleaning audio, and structuring the video.

Day 4: Editing (Part 2). Add finishing touches like captions, music, or simple visuals. Export the final video.

Day 5: Uploading & Optimization. Create or finalize the thumbnail, write the description, add tags, add end screens, and schedule the video.

Day 6: Promotion & Engagement. Share the video on one or two platforms and respond to comments.

Day 7: Rest or Review. Check analytics briefly, note what worked, then step away. Rest is part of consistency.

This rhythm spreads the workload, reduces burnout, and makes it easier to stay consistent long-term.

Why These Timetables Matter

Neither schedule is better. The right one is the one you can repeat without resentment. Consistency isn't about squeezing YouTube into every free minute; it's about designing a workflow that respects your time, energy, and life.

Your Action Steps for Today

1. Map out your version of consistency. Sketch a realistic **YouTube workflow** that fits your current life. List the main tasks, from planning to publishing, and decide whether you'd rather do them all at once or spread them out.

2. Estimate your time honestly. Roughly estimate how long each step might take. This helps prevent overcommitting and makes future planning easier.

3. Choose a pace you can repeat. Decide what consistency means for you right now, weekly, biweekly, or monthly, and commit to that rhythm rather than an idealized version of productivity.

Optional Reflection

Write down one reason you're creating content that has nothing to do with views or money. Keep it somewhere visible. When motivation dips, that reminder can bring you back to center.

Tomorrow, we'll focus on working smarter, not harder, by building systems that let you batch, repurpose, and streamline your content without losing your creative spark.

Day 28: Working Smarter: Systems for Batching, Repurposing, and Automation

By now, you've probably felt it: YouTube isn't just about creativity; it's also about time management. Planning, filming, editing, uploading, promoting, and engaging all add up, and if you treat every video as a completely new project, burnout comes quickly. The good news is that you don't need to work harder to grow. You need systems that reduce friction. In 2026, sustainable creators don't rely on motivation alone; they rely on **batching, repurposing, and automation** to protect their time and energy while staying consistent. Today is about shifting from doing everything manually to building workflows that support you.

Batching: Create Once, Free Up Your Time Later

Batching simply means grouping similar tasks together instead of constantly switching between them. Your brain works more efficiently when it stays in the same mode for longer periods. Instead of planning one video today, filming it tomorrow, editing it the next day, and repeating that cycle over and over, batching lets you stack tasks. You might outline several videos in one sitting, film them all in one setup session, and then edit them across a few shorter sessions later. The biggest benefit of batching isn't speed; it's mental relief. Your camera is already set up, your lighting is already right, and you are already **in creator mode.** That momentum matters. Batching also gives you breathing room. When life gets busy or motivation dips, having content ready prevents gaps that can quietly derail consistency. You don't need to batch an entire month. Even filming two videos in one session is enough to feel the difference.

Repurposing: Let One Video Do More Work

Repurposing is about maximizing the value of what you already create. You've already done the hardest part: thinking, filming, and explaining. Repurposing simply lets that effort travel further. A single long-form YouTube video can become short vertical clips, quotes, graphics, summaries, or behind-the-scenes posts. Each format reaches people who consume content differently, without requiring you to reinvent anything. This approach also removes pressure. You're not constantly asking, "What do I post today?" You're asking, "How else can this already-made content help someone?"

The Repurposing Workflow

You don't need to be on every platform. Instead, choose one or two formats that feel natural and let your content multiply. Here is how one ten-minute video can become a week of posts:

- **Short-Form Clips (Shorts, Reels, TikTok):** Use YouTube's built-in **Edit into a Short** tool or AI-clipping software (like **OpusClip** or **CapCut**) to find the viral moments. Focus on fifteen- to thirty-second highlights with high-energy hooks.
- **Written Takeaways (X, Threads, LinkedIn):** Take the **main lesson** from your video and turn it into a text-based thread or a professional post. People often prefer to read a quick summary before committing to a full video.
- **Community Updates:** Share a **Behind-the-Scenes** photo or a blooper from the shoot on your **Community Tab**. This builds a personal connection that a polished video can't always reach.
- **The Newsletter Deep Dive:** If you have an email list, use your video script as the foundation for your weekly newsletter. Simply polish the text, add a few images, and link back to the video.

Repurposing doesn't mean being everywhere. It means choosing one or two formats that feel natural and letting your content quietly multiply.

Automation: Reduce Repetition, Not Creativity

Automation isn't about removing the human element; it's about removing unnecessary repetition so your creativity has more room to breathe. Many parts of YouTube are predictable. Your descriptions usually include the same links. Your titles often follow familiar patterns. Your upload settings rarely change. When you automate these elements, you're not cutting corners; you're protecting your attention and energy. One of the easiest places to start is **YouTube Studio's Upload Defaults**. This lets you pre-fill things like your standard description, social links, affiliate disclaimers, tags, and visibility settings. Instead of rewriting the same information every time, it appears automatically when you upload a new video. You can always tweak it, but you're never starting from scratch.

How to Set Up YouTube Studio Upload Defaults

- Select **YouTube Studio**.
- In the left-hand sidebar, scroll down and click on **Settings**.
- In the pop-up window, choose **Upload defaults**.

Under the Basic Info tab:

- Add a reusable **description block** (channel intro, social links, affiliate disclaimer, call to action).
- Insert default **tags** related to your niche or recurring topics.
- Include anything you normally copy and paste into every description.

Under the Advanced Settings tab:

- Choose your default comment settings (allow comments, hold for review, etc.).
- Mark whether your videos usually include paid promotions.
- Select a default visibility setting (Private, Unlisted, or Public).
- Click **Save** to apply your defaults.

From now on, every new upload will automatically include these settings. You can still customize each video individually, but you'll never have to start from a blank page again. This small setup step saves time, reduces mental load, and makes staying consistent much easier.

Templates are another powerful form of automation. A simple video outline template can include sections like hook, main points, examples, and call to action. A title template might follow formats like "How to ___ Without ___" or "The Truth About ___." Thumbnail templates help you stay visually consistent while saving design time. These don't limit creativity. They remove friction so you can focus on the message instead of formatting.

Checklists are where automation really shines for beginners. Create one checklist for filming, one for editing, and one for uploading. Your filming checklist might include camera battery, mic levels, framing, and lighting. Your editing checklist could include trimming dead space, adding captions, and checking audio levels. Your upload checklist might cover thumbnails, descriptions, end screens, and pinned comments. When your brain is tired, the checklist carries the load.

You can also automate small but time-saving actions outside of YouTube. Scheduling tools like **Meta Business Suite** or **Buffer** let you queue social posts in advance instead of posting manually every time. Text expanders or saved replies can speed up common responses to comments or emails. Even something as simple as keeping a **copy-paste folder** with your most-used links and phrases can shave minutes off every upload.

Over time, these systems compound. What starts as saving five minutes here and ten minutes there becomes hours reclaimed every month. That extra time doesn't have to go into producing more content: it can go into better ideas, clearer delivery, rest, or simply enjoying the process again.

Automation doesn't make your channel robotic. It makes it sustainable. And sustainability is what allows creativity to last. But remember: systems are the skeleton, not the heart. While automation handles the repetitive tasks, your focus should remain on the art of the video itself.

The Athlete Mindset: Loving the Craft

As you begin to build systems to make your workflow more efficient, it's easy to start looking for shortcuts that remove the work entirely. However, there is a common trait among top creators who have lasted for over a decade: **they are obsessed with the craft.**

The Athlete Analogy

Think of a professional athlete. They don't just show up for the game on Sunday; they actually enjoy the hours of practice, the film study, and the weight room. In the same way, the creators who find long-term success are those who enjoy the process of storytelling, the puzzle of editing, or the challenge of framing a perfect shot.

- **Longevity Requires Love:** Efficiency helps you stay organized, but if you genuinely hate the process and are only chasing a **viral**

outcome, you will eventually run out of energy. You have to like the work enough to do it even on the days when the views are low.
- **Systems vs. Shortcuts:** A system is designed to help you do the work better; a shortcut is designed to help you avoid the work. Top creators use systems to clear away the **boring** stuff (by automation) so they can spend more time on the **fun** stuff (the creative craft).

Why Obsession Wins

When you care about the craft, your **quality floor** rises. You stop asking, "What is the bare minimum I can do to get this video out?" and start asking, "How can I make this transition a little smoother?" or "How can I make this explanation even clearer?" That obsession is what viewers eventually feel, and it's what keeps them coming back. Don't build systems just to save time; build them to save your energy for the parts of the craft you love. Efficiency gets you to the finish line, but obsession keeps you coming back to the starting blocks.

Why This Matters More Than Hustle

Posting more doesn't automatically mean growing more. What matters is **showing up consistently for the love of the craft while ensuring that you don't exhaust yourself**. Viewers build trust around rhythm. When they know what to expect weekly, biweekly, or monthly, they're more likely to return. The algorithm also favors predictability because it helps keep audiences engaged over time. When your workflow depends entirely on last-minute effort, consistency breaks easily. Systems are what keep you going when motivation is low, energy is limited, or life gets complicated. Working smarter isn't about cutting corners. It's about making YouTube fit into your life instead of competing with it.

Your Action Steps for Today

1. Choose one system to try this week. Decide whether batching, repurposing, or automation would help you most right now, and focus on just one.

2. Apply it in a small way. You might outline two videos at once, turn one existing clip into a Short, or set up upload defaults in YouTube Studio. Small changes count.

3. Notice the difference. Pay attention to how it affects your stress, time, and motivation. Systems only work if they actually make your life easier.

Optional Reflection

Which part of your process feels the most draining right now? What would change if that step required half the effort next time? What can you automate next so you can focus more on your creativity?

Tomorrow, we'll zoom out and talk about **long-term improvement** and how the **Rule of 100** mindset helps creators get better with every upload without chasing perfection.

Day 29: The Rule of 100 (Reframed for Modern YouTube)

If there's one mindset that consistently separates creators who grow from creators who quit, it's this: stop chasing perfection and start building momentum. Your early videos are not supposed to be great. They're supposed to exist. YouTube rewards creators who show up, learn quickly, and improve steadily, not those who wait endlessly for the **perfect** idea, setup, or moment. Every upload is feedback. Every upload is practice. Every upload moves you forward. That's where the **Rule of 100** comes in: not as pressure, but as permission.

What the Rule of 100 Really Means

The **Rule of 100** is simple: commit to making 100 videos, with the understanding that improvement comes through repetition and reflection, not instant success. This does **not** mean uploading 100 videos as fast as possible. It means releasing yourself from the unrealistic expectation that any single video has to **make it.** Instead, each video becomes one step in a longer process. Think of it like training. You don't expect strength from one workout. You expect it from showing up consistently and learning what works over time. By the time you reach your 50th or 100th upload, you will naturally be better at:

- Writing stronger hooks and openings.
- Speaking with confidence on camera.
- Editing faster and cleaner.
- Understanding pacing and structure.
- Choosing better topics and titles.
- Reading audience signals and feedback.
- Developing a recognizable style.

None of that happens overnight. It happens through repetition.

Progress Beats Perfection (Every Time)

One of the most common hurdles for new creators is treating every single upload like a final exam. When you put that much pressure on yourself, every video feels like a high-stakes test, which inevitably leads to hesitation, creative blocks, and eventually, burnout.

To combat this, rely on **the Rule of 100**. This mindset reframes your first 100 videos not as a portfolio of masterpieces but as a series of essential practice sessions. Instead of asking yourself, "Will this video go viral?" or "Is this perfect?" you shift your focus to a much more productive question: "What is the one thing I can improve this time?"

By narrowing your focus, you can make steady, manageable progress in areas like:

- **Audio Clarity:** Perhaps you try a different room or adjust your microphone settings.
- **A Tighter Intro:** You practice getting to the point five seconds faster than last time.
- **Confident Delivery:** You focus on making more **eye contact** with the camera lens.
- **Visual Storytelling:** You experiment with one simple B-roll clip or a basic text overlay.
- **Pacing:** You cut out a few more "ums" and "ahs" in the edit.

The secret to long-term success on YouTube is **compounding interest.** You don't need to fix every flaw at once. If you improve just 1% with every video, you will be a completely different (and much more skilled) creator by the time you hit video twenty, fifty, or one hundred. Give yourself the permission to be a **work in progress**; it is the only way to eventually become an expert.

How to Learn From Each Upload (Without Obsessing)

You don't need to drown in analytics to improve. A simple reflection habit is enough.

After each video, take a few minutes to ask:

- What felt stronger in this video compared to the last one?
- Where did viewers start dropping off?
- Did the title and thumbnail match the content clearly?
- What kind of comments or feedback did I receive?
- Would I click this if it showed up in my feed?

This isn't about self-criticism. It's about curiosity. Curiosity leads to clarity, and clarity leads to growth.

The Compounding Power of Your Video Library

By the time you reach your 100th video, you will stop thinking about **views per video** and start thinking about your **Content Catalog.** In 2026, YouTube is the world's most powerful **evergreen** platform. On apps like TikTok or Instagram, a post disappears in hours. On YouTube, your video is a **permanent book** on a **digital shelf** that people can discover for years.

- **The Library Effect:** Every new video you publish acts as a new **front door** to your channel. A viewer might find you through a video you made today, but then they **binge** three videos you made six months ago. More videos mean more opportunities for the algorithm to match you with a viewer.
- **Passive Discovery:** In your first month, you have to work hard for every single view. By your 50th or 100th video, your older content is often generating more views and subscribers than your newest upload. This is **compounding growth;** your past work supports your future success.
- **A Safety Net for Revenue:** Every video in your library is like a tiny employee. One might be earning ad revenue, another is generating affiliate sales, and a third is building trust. The larger your **staff** (your catalog), the more stable your creative business becomes.

The Takeaway: Don't judge your success solely by how your latest video performed in its first twenty-four hours. Judge it by the total size of your library. Each upload is a brick in a foundation that gets stronger and more discoverable over time.

Every Creator You Admire Started Rough

If you scroll back far enough on almost any successful channel, you'll find awkward intros, shaky camera work, uneven pacing, and videos the creator would never upload today. Those early videos didn't succeed because they were good. They succeeded because they existed.

Most creators who eventually grow don't see meaningful traction at video five or ten. Many don't feel momentum until video twenty-five, fifty, or later. The difference is that they stayed long enough to improve.

Growth Includes Change (And That's a Good Thing)

Your niche will evolve. Your style will sharpen. Your confidence will grow. You may look back at your early uploads and cringe, and that's actually a sign of progress. Changing direction, refining your format, or adjusting your strategy isn't failure. It's feedback in action. The Rule of 100 gives you permission to evolve without guilt.

Your Action Step for Today

Start a simple Creator Log, a document, notebook, or note on your phone, and use it after every upload to track growth. After each video, write down:

- The video title or topic
- One thing you intentionally improved this time
- One thing that worked better than expected
- One thing you want to improve next

Tip: Focus on improving just **one element per video**. Consistent small upgrades create massive long-term growth.

Optional Reflection

If you committed to creating 100 videos, one step at a time, where could you realistically be a year from now? Not just in numbers, but in confidence, skill, and clarity.

Tomorrow, we'll wrap up the 30-day journey by helping you reflect on how far you've come, what you've learned about yourself as a creator, and the direction you want your channel to grow from here.

Day 30: Your Post-Launch Growth Plan

You Did It!

Over the past thirty days, you moved from intention to action. You didn't just think about starting a YouTube channel; you built one. You planned, filmed, uploaded, promoted, analyzed, and showed up. That alone puts you ahead of the vast majority of people who never move past the idea stage.

Whether you uploaded one video or several, whether your numbers feel exciting or underwhelming, the most important truth is this: your channel is no longer theoretical. It exists. And now, you get to decide what it becomes.

This final day isn't about closing a chapter. It's about shifting gears: from launching to growing.

You Don't Need the Whole Plan; Just the Next Step

YouTube in 2026 is constantly evolving. Algorithms change. Features update. Trends rise and fall. No creator, no matter how experienced, has everything figured out. The goal moving forward isn't certainty; it's direction.

Take a moment to reflect on what you've learned so far:

- What kind of content felt most natural or energizing to create?
- Which parts of the process felt easier than expected, and which felt heavy?
- What upload rhythm actually fits your real life right now?
- What skill would make the biggest difference if you improved it next?

You don't need perfect answers. You just need enough clarity to take the next step with intention.

What to Prioritize After the Launch Phase

Once the excitement of launching fades, growth becomes about habits, not hype.

Consistency matters more than intensity. Posting weekly, biweekly, or even monthly can work if it's predictable and realistic for you. Viewers build trust when they know what to expect, and YouTube favors channels that show up regularly over time. Consistency isn't about grinding; it's about building a rhythm you can sustain.

Experimentation should remain part of your process. Try different formats, adjust your pacing, test new hooks, or explore slightly different topics within your niche. Not every experiment will work, but every one teaches you something useful.

The community deserves attention early. Replies, comments, and conversations create loyalty long before numbers explode. A small, engaged audience is far more powerful than a large, silent one. Treat YouTube as a conversation, not a broadcast.

Your creative energy is a resource: protect it. Burnout ends more channels than lack of skill ever will. Rest, boundaries, and flexibility aren't weaknesses; they're part of staying creative long-term.

Honoring Your Creative Season

One of the most dangerous myths on YouTube is that there is only one correct way to grow. You might hear people say you **must** post every week or you'll fail. In reality, the best strategy is the one that fits your current life. Success isn't about ignoring your real world for your channel; it's about making smart trade-offs. You want to still be creating five years from now, not just for the next five weeks. To do that, you need to recognize which season you are in:

1. The Sprint Season (High Energy)

This is when you have extra time, high motivation, and fewer outside responsibilities.

- **The Goal:** Build momentum.
- **The Strategy:** This is the time to **go all in**. Experiment with new styles, record multiple videos in one day (batching), and push yourself to learn new skills quickly. If you have the wind at your back, use it to gain as much ground as possible.

2. The Maintenance Season (Life Happens)

You might be starting a new job, moving house, or caring for family. Your **mental battery** is being used elsewhere.

- **The Goal:** Stay in the game.
- **The Strategy:** Don't try to sprint when you're tired. Instead of a long, complex video every week, maybe you could post one high-quality short every ten days or move to a biweekly schedule. The win here isn't **explosive growth**; it's simply not stopping.

3. The Pivot Season (The Shift)

Sometimes, the niche you chose just doesn't excite you anymore. You feel stuck or bored with your own content.

- **The Goal:** Find your spark again.
- **The Strategy:** Give yourself permission to slow down and explore. Test a completely different topic or a new filming style. Don't worry about the **perfect** result; just focus on what makes you curious. A pivot isn't a failure; it's an evolution.

The Takeaway: Your priorities will shift, and that is okay. If you try to force a **Sprint** during a **Maintenance** season, you will burn out and quit. True consistency isn't doing the same thing forever; it's choosing the pace that fits the life you are actually living right now. **It is better to walk for a year than to run for a week and collapse.**

And finally, shift your goals from outcomes to actions. Subscriber counts and views fluctuate. Habits don't. Goals like uploading one video every two weeks, batching content once a month, or responding to comments for the first day after posting give you control over your progress.

If You Still Feel Unsure, You're Not Behind

Feeling uncertain doesn't mean you're failing; it means you're early. Every creator, no matter how established, goes through cycles of doubt, plateau, and reinvention. The difference between those who grow and those who stop is simple: they keep going anyway.

This guide isn't something you finish and forget. Come back to it when you need grounding. Revisit earlier days. Compare your first uploads to your latest ones. Progress is often clearer in hindsight.

Your channel is not a one-time project. It's an evolving system: one that grows as you do.

Your Action Steps for Today

1. Write down three specific things you accomplished during these thirty days, no matter how small they seem. Take a moment to acknowledge what you've built.

2. Then choose one clear next step:

- Outline your next three video ideas.
- Create a simple weekly or biweekly upload plan.
- Set a personal thirty-day challenge that feels achievable.
- Define what kind of creator you want to be one year from now, not just in numbers, but in values, style, and confidence.

This is your reset point. Not the end, just the beginning of a smarter, steadier phase. Thank yourself for showing up. For learning in public. For building something from nothing.

Your channel is live. Your foundation is set. And your growth starts now.

Bonus Section: Resources to Help You Create With Confidence

This bonus section is your long-term support system, designed to help you long after the thirty-day launch is complete. As your channel grows, your needs will change, and this toolkit is here to grow with you.

Inside, you'll find practical checklists, templates, and reference guides you can return to at any stage of your creator journey. Whether you're planning your next batch of videos, reviewing analytics, organizing your finances, or refining your workflow, these resources are built to save time, reduce overwhelm, and support consistent progress.

Think of this section as your reset button. Come back whenever you need clarity, structure, or momentum. You don't need to reinvent your process each time; these tools exist so you can focus on what matters most: creating with intention, improving with each upload, and building something sustainable over time.

Essential YouTube & Creator Tools

Practical apps, platforms, and software to support your creator journey in 2026.

This is a curated, beginner-friendly toolkit you can grow into over time. You don't need everything on this list. Start with the tools that fit your budget, comfort level, and content style, then upgrade only when a clear need appears. Many successful creators begin with free tools and add paid ones later as their workflow and income evolve.

Recommended pairing: Especially useful alongside **Days 9–12** (***Building Your Creator Setup***) and throughout Weeks Three and Four.

Video Recording & Editing

- **CapCut (Free + Paid):** An intuitive editor for mobile and desktop. Excellent for Shorts, Reels, TikToks, and clean long-form cuts. Includes templates, captions, and basic effects. Paid plans unlock advanced assets.
- **iMovie (Free – Apple only):** A simple, reliable editor for iPhone, iPad, and Mac users. Ideal for first videos and straightforward edits without a learning curve.
- **DaVinci Resolve (Free + Paid):** A professional-grade editor with powerful color correction and audio tools. The free version is extremely capable; the paid version adds advanced features for scaling creators.
- **Adobe Premiere Pro (Paid):** An industry standard for long-form editing. Very powerful, integrates with other Adobe tools, but best for creators who are ready to invest time and money.
- **OBS Studio (Free):** Widely used for screen recording and live streaming. Popular for tutorials, gaming, and presentations. Steeper setup, but very flexible.

Thumbnails & Graphic Design

- **Canva (Free + Paid):** One of the most beginner-friendly tools for thumbnails, banners, Shorts covers, and social media posts. Templates make branding consistent; Pro unlocks premium assets.

- **Adobe Express (Free + Paid):** Fast, clean design tool with ready-made thumbnail and social media templates. Great if you want something lighter than full Adobe apps.
- **Pixlr (Free):** A lightweight browser editor for quick thumbnail tweaks, cropping, and text overlays.
- **Remove.bg (Free + Paid):** Automatically removes backgrounds from photos. Perfect for face cutouts in thumbnails.

Keywords, SEO & Optimization

- **TubeBuddy (Free + Paid):** Browser extension for keyword research, tag suggestions, bulk edits, and A/B testing thumbnails and titles. Especially useful for improving CTR.
- **VidIQ (Free + Paid):** Keyword insights, trend alerts, competitive analysis, and daily idea prompts. Helpful for topic research and early optimization.
- **Google Trends (Free):** Shows how interest in topics changes over time. Great for validating video ideas and spotting seasonal trends.
- **AnswerThePublic (Free + Paid):** Reveals real questions people ask around a topic: excellent for titles, hooks, and evergreen content ideas.

Music & Sound Effects

- **YouTube Audio Library (Free):** Safe, royalty-free music and sound effects approved for YouTube monetization.
- **Epidemic Sound (Paid):** High-quality music with a creator-friendly license. Popular with vloggers and long-form creators.
- **Artlist (Paid):** Unlimited downloads with a single subscription, covering commercial use across platforms.
- **Freesound (Free, attribution often required):** Community-driven sound effects library. Always check the license before use.

Productivity, Planning & Systems

- **Notion (Free + Paid):** An all-in-one workspace for scripts, content calendars, creator logs, and monetization tracking. Extremely flexible.

- **Trello (Free + Paid):** Visual boards for managing video stages (idea → filmed → edited → published).
- **Google Drive (Free + Paid):** Docs for scripts, Sheets for analytics or finances, and Drive for asset storage.
- **Airtable (Free + Paid):** A hybrid spreadsheet-database for tracking videos, sponsors, or affiliate links at scale.

Analytics & Growth Tracking

- **YouTube Studio (Free):** Your main control center: analytics, comments, monetization, uploads, organic vs. paid performance, and collaborations.
- **Social Blade (Free + Paid):** Provides public growth estimates and trend comparisons. Helpful for understanding general growth patterns, but not precise.
- **Monetization, Links & Support Tools**
- **Bitly (Free + Paid):** Shortens and tracks links for descriptions, bios, and affiliate URLs.
- **Ko-fi (Free + Paid) / Buy Me a Coffee (Free + Paid):** Let viewers support you with tips or memberships, useful before full monetization.
- **Linktree / Beacons / Solo.to (Free + Paid):** Create one clean link that holds your videos, socials, affiliate links, and products.
- **Google Workspace (Free + Paid):** Set up a professional email (e.g., hello@yourchannel.com) for brands and collaborations.

Live Streaming & Community (New in 2026)

- **YouTube Live (Free):** Includes **Practice Before Live**, vertical live streaming, and AI-generated live highlights that can become Shorts, ideal for building community without extra editing.
- **StreamYard (Free + Paid):** Browser-based live streaming with guests, overlays, and branding, great for interviews and panels.

Final Tip: You don't need the **perfect stack** to succeed. Start with what's free and familiar. As your channel grows, let your workflow, not trends, decide which tools you add next. The best tools are the ones that reduce friction and help you keep creating.

Monthly Content & Upload Planner

Turn your ideas into a realistic upload habit.

By adopting a smarter planning system and maintaining a consistent publishing schedule, you can significantly reduce last-minute pressure and ensure your creative process remains enjoyable and sustainable.

This planner is designed to help you see your entire month at a glance: what you're making, when you're making it, and how everything fits into your life. It's especially useful if you're balancing YouTube with work, school, or other commitments, because it encourages realistic pacing instead of pressure.

You can recreate this planner in Notion, Google Sheets, or Airtable, or print it and fill it in by hand. The format is flexible; the goal is clarity, not perfection.

Recommended use: Pair with **Day 14** (***Practice Day***) for short-term planning and **Day 30** (***Your Post-Launch Growth Plan***) for long-term consistency.

Monthly Planning Snapshot

Monthly Calendar Overview

Week	Video Title	Script/ Outline	Film date	Edit Date	Upload Date
1					
2					
3					
4					

Month: ____________________

Primary focus or theme this month: ____________________

Upload frequency goal (e.g., weekly, biweekly): ______________

____

Monthly Focus Prompts (Optional but Powerful)

At the start of each month, take five minutes to answer these:

This month's main creative focus (one sentence):

Number of videos I realistically want to publish:

One skill I want to improve this month (hook, pacing, thumbnail clarity, storytelling):

Any key dates, holidays, launches, or events to plan around:

Potential collaboration, live stream, or experiment I want to try:

End-of-Month Reflection

At the end of the month, review your planner and jot down quick notes:

What went smoothly this month?

What felt rushed or stressful?

One thing I'll simplify next month:

One thing I'll repeat because it worked:

Tips for Using This Planner Well

Choose your upload day or days first, then build everything else around those anchors. Consistency comes from predictability, not volume. Use simple symbols or colors to track progress, such as planned, filmed, edited, scheduled, and published, so you can see momentum at a glance. Leave intentional white space in your calendar. Overflow weeks are normal and often necessary.

Most importantly, treat this planner as a support system, not a rulebook. You don't need to upload constantly to grow. You need a plan you can return to every month, one that helps you stay focused, creative, and steady over time.

Weekly Content Workflow Planner

Batch smarter. Stay consistent. Reduce creative stress.

This weekly overview is designed for creators who want structure without rigidity. Instead of reacting day by day, you map the entire week in advance, so filming, editing, and publishing feel intentional rather than overwhelming.

This template works especially well if you create **one to two long-form videos per week**, with optional Shorts or promotional content layered in. You can print it, recreate it in Notion or Google Sheets, or adapt it inside any planner you already use.

Recommended use: Best paired with **Day 28 (*Working Smarter: Batching, Repurposing, and Automation)***

Day	Video Title / Topic	Script / Outline	Film	Edit	Upload	Promote	Notes
Monday	Video 1 + Video 2 Planning	Script Video 1 + Video 2					Research keywords & outlines
Tuesday		Script Video 1 + Video 2					Research keywords & outlines
Wednesday			Film Videos 1 + 2				B-roll or retakes as needed
Thursday				Edit Video 1			Aim for 70% completion of Video 1 edit
Friday				Edit Video 2	Upload Video 1		Schedule Video 1
Saturday					Upload Video 2	Promote both videos	Post to social + respond to comments
Sunday							Reflect & prep next week's topics

How to Use This Template Effectively

This is a batching framework, not a rulebook. You can move days around to match your energy or availability. Some creators film everything in one day. Others split filming across shorter sessions. The goal is to reduce switching between tasks and forced productivity. Having two videos in progress at once creates flexibility. If life gets busy, you still have momentum. If you only publish one video per week, simply stretch this schedule across two weeks.

"Promotion" doesn't mean shouting links everywhere. It can be as simple as posting one Short, replying to comments, or adding a Community post.

Weekly Planning Prompts (Optional but Powerful)

Use these at the start of each week to stay focused:

- Main theme or focus this week: ________________________
  ____
- Number of long-form videos planned: __________________
  ____
- Short-form goal (clips, Shorts, Reels): ________________
  ____
- One skill to improve this week (hook, pacing, thumbnail, etc.):
  ____
- Any collaborations, trends, or events to account for:
  ____

Consistency doesn't come from doing more. It comes from deciding once how your week works and letting the system carry you.

This template isn't about hustle. It's about clarity, rhythm, and sustainability.

Video Production Checklist for YouTube

A step-by-step checklist to take every video from idea to upload.

Use this checklist before every upload to stay consistent and avoid missing important steps. You can print it, copy it into Notion or Google Docs, or reuse it as a template for every video.

1. PLAN THE VIDEO

☐ Choose a clear topic or question.
☐ Do basic keyword research (YouTube search, Google, TubeBuddy, VidIQ).
☐ Draft a working title (can refine later).
☐ Outline the video structure (hook, main points, ending).
☐ Decide what B-roll, examples, or visuals are needed.
☐ Check the filming setup (lighting, background, outfit).
☐ Gather props, gear, or screen recordings.

2. FILM THE VIDEO

☐ Set up the camera and lighting (phone is fine).
☐ Record a short test clip for audio and framing.
☐ Film the main footage (A-roll).
☐ Capture B-roll, cutaways, or screen recordings.
☐ Speak clearly and with energy.
☐ Review the footage before ending the session.

3. EDIT THE VIDEO

☐ Import and organize clips.
☐ Trim mistakes, filler words, and long pauses.
☐ Insert B-roll or cutaways.
☐ Add text, music, or effects if helpful.
☐ Check pacing and audio levels.
☐ Export the final video.

☐ Watch the full export once.

4. OPTIMIZE BEFORE UPLOADING

☐ Design or select the thumbnail.
☐ Finalize the title (clear promise, not clickbait).
☐ Write the description (summary, links, CTA).
☐ Add relevant tags.
☐ Choose a playlist (if applicable).
☐ Add end screens and cards.
☐ Add captions or subtitles (optional)

5. UPLOAD & SHARE

☐ Upload the video to YouTube.
☐ Double-check the title, description, thumbnail, and tags.
☐ Select audience settings (kids / not for kids).
☐ Set visibility (public, unlisted, scheduled).
☐ Publish or schedule.
☐ Share on selected platforms or with friends.
☐ Respond to early comments.

6. REVIEW & REFLECT

☐ Check the video's performance in YouTube Studio.
☐ Review CTR, retention, and traffic sources.
☐ Note one thing that worked well.
☐ Note one thing to improve next time.
☐ Log insights in your Creator Log or Reflection Tracker.

Reminder: This checklist is a system, not a test. Each time you use it, the process gets faster, and your videos get better.

Video Reflection Tracker

Learn faster by reflecting smarter: one upload at a time.

This tracker is designed to help you improve steadily without being overwhelmed. Instead of chasing perfection or obsessing over analytics, you use each upload as feedback. One video. One lesson. One clear improvement. Use this reflection tracker **after every published video,** whether it performed well or not. Over time, these entries become a powerful record of your growth as a creator.

You can print one page per video, duplicate it digitally in Notion or Google Docs, or keep it as an ongoing journal.

Recommended use: Best paired with **Day 29:** ***The Rule of 100 (Reframed for Modern YouTube)***

Video Reflection Entry

Video title / topic: ____

Date published: ____

Link (optional): ____

Format: Long-form / Short / Live / Repurposed

Video length: ____

1. What Worked Well in This Video?

Be specific. Focus on strengths, not vague positives.

Examples: the hook felt clearer, pacing improved, the audio was cleaner, the editing felt faster, and the energy felt more natural.

____

____

2. One Thing I Intentionally Tried or Changed

This helps you connect effort to outcome.

Examples: new hook style, faster intro, different thumbnail layout, tighter cuts, less scripting.

___

___

3. One Thing to Improve Next Time (Only One)

Choose **one** focused upgrade. This keeps progress sustainable.

Examples: lighting consistency, confidence on camera, smoother transitions, clearer CTA, stronger thumbnail contrast.

___

___

4. Early Viewer Response & Signals

Look lightly at feedback: not judgment, just information.

• Any notable comments or questions?

• Retention dips or strong moments?

• Is CTR higher or lower than usual?

___

___

5. Insight to Carry Forward

What lesson does this video teach you for the next one?

This is the most important section.

___

___

Optional Add-On: Shorts & Repurposing Notes

If this video was clipped or repurposed, consider the following:

- Did any Short outperform expectations?
- Was there a moment viewers rewatched or shared?

____

____

Reminder for Creators

Growth doesn't come from fixing everything. It comes from **noticing one thing** and doing it slightly better next time. Stack enough small improvements, and the channel changes quietly, steadily, and sustainably.

YouTube Analytics Glossary

Master the metrics that drive discovery.

Recommended use: Best paired with **Day 22: *Reading Analytics Without Overthinking Them***

Below is a clean, alphabetical glossary designed for quick reference. The language is intentionally plain so you can understand your data without needing a marketing or analytics background.

Average Percentage Viewed: The average portion of your video that viewers watch. For example, if your video is ten minutes long and viewers watch six minutes on average, your average percentage viewed is 60%. This is a strong indicator of pacing and content clarity.

Average View Duration (AVD): The average amount of time viewers spend watching your video. It's calculated by dividing total watch time by total views. Higher AVD usually means your content is engaging and well-paced.

Audience Retention: A visual graph showing where viewers stay, skip ahead, rewatch, or leave your video. Spikes suggest moments of interest; drops point to confusion, slow pacing, or unmet expectations.

Click-Through Rate (CTR): The percentage of people who clicked on your video after seeing the thumbnail and title. CTR = Clicks ÷ Impressions. For newer channels, 4–10% is considered healthy. CTR reflects **packaging**, not content quality.

Device Type: Shows what devices viewers are using (TV, mobile, desktop, tablet). With TV viewership growing fast, this can influence how large text, visuals, and pacing should be.

Engaged Views: Measures views where viewers watched long enough to meaningfully engage. This metric helps distinguish casual clicks from real interest, especially for Shorts and promoted content.

Engagement: Includes likes, comments, shares, and other interactions. Engagement signals to YouTube that your video is valuable and worth recommending to more viewers.

First Thirty Seconds Retention: Shows how many viewers remain after the opening moments of your video. Strong videos often retain 85–90% of viewers here. Big drops usually mean the hook didn't deliver.

Impressions: The number of times your thumbnail was shown on YouTube (Home, Search, Suggested, etc.). Impressions tell you how often YouTube is putting your content in front of people.

Impressions Click-Through Rate: CTR calculated only from impressions shown in major discovery areas like Home, Search, and Suggested videos. This is one of the clearest indicators of whether your video attracts attention at scale.

Key Moments for Audience Retention: Automatically highlights moments where viewers drop off, skip ahead, or replay. This makes it easier to diagnose weak intros, confusing sections, or standout moments without manually scrubbing graphs.

New Viewers: People who are discovering your channel for the first time. Growth depends on attracting new viewers while converting some into returning ones.

Organic Performance (new reporting split): Shows how your video performs naturally through Search, Browse, Suggested, and subscriptions, without paid promotion. This reflects pure content-quality signals.

Paid Performance (new reporting split): Shows how your video performs when promoted through ads or YouTube Promote. Paid performance is influenced by targeting and budget, not the recommendation algorithm.

Returning Viewers: Viewers who have watched your channel before. An increase here signals loyalty and community building rather than one-off clicks.

Revenue Reports (monetized channels only)*:* Includes estimated earnings, RPM (revenue per 1,000 views), and income sources such as ads, memberships, and fan funding. Revenue data appears only after joining YPP.

Subscribers Gained / Lost: Tracks how many subscribers a specific video attracts or causes to unsubscribe. This helps you understand which content strengthens or weakens audience trust.

Subscriber Count: The total number of people subscribed to your channel. Useful to track over time, but best viewed alongside watch time and retention rather than alone.

Top Moments: Peaks in the retention graph where viewers rewatch or rewind. These moments often reveal your strongest storytelling, clarity, or emotional beats.

Top Videos: Your highest-performing videos by views or watch time. These are clues to what topics, formats, or titles resonate most with your audience.

Traffic Sources: Shows how viewers found your video: search, suggested, browse (home), external links, or social platforms. This helps you understand which discovery paths are working.

Unique Viewers: An estimate of how many different people watched your content over a given period. Useful for understanding reach rather than repeat watching.

Views: The number of times your video was watched. A view typically counts after roughly thirty seconds (or the full video if it's shorter). Views show reach, but not depth of engagement.

Views per Unique Viewer: Shows how often, on average, each viewer watches your content. Higher numbers suggest strong interest or rewatch value.

Watch Time (Hours): The total amount of time viewers have spent watching your videos. This is one of the strongest signals YouTube uses to decide what to recommend.

Watch Time from Impressions: How much watch time resulted specifically from people clicking after seeing your thumbnail. This connects packaging directly to real engagement.

Conclusion: From Starting to Sustaining

If you take nothing else from this book, take this: You are no longer a beginner who **wants** to start a YouTube channel. You are a creator who **has started**. That distinction matters more than any algorithm update, tool, or strategy.

Over the past thirty days, you didn't just learn how YouTube works; you built something real. You moved from hesitation to action, from theory to practice. You planned, filmed, edited, uploaded, reflected, and improved. You learned how to work with the platform instead of feeling intimidated by it. Most importantly, you proved to yourself that you can show up, learn in public, and keep going.

That's the hardest part. And you've already done it.

What You've Actually Built

This book wasn't designed to turn you into a viral sensation overnight. It was designed to give you something far more valuable: **a foundation that lasts**.

You now have:

- A repeatable workflow for creating videos.
- A clear understanding of how YouTube evaluates content.

- Systems for planning, batching, and improving.
- The confidence to upload imperfect work.
- The awareness to read analytics without spiraling.
- The mindset to grow steadily instead of burning out.

Those are skills, and skills compound over time.

In the ever-evolving world of YouTube, views will fluctuate, algorithms will shift, and new tools will emerge every year. However, the technical and creative skills you build during this process are yours to keep forever.

The real secret to success on YouTube isn't just growth; it is **continuity**. Most channels don't fade away because the creator lacks talent or potential. Instead, they disappear simply because the creator stops. They might stop after the initial discomfort of their first "awkward" video or when they face a season of low views. Often, they stop when the initial spark of motivation fades or when life simply gets too busy.

This book was designed to help you avoid that specific outcome. In 2026, consistency no longer means feeling forced to post constantly at the expense of your well-being. Instead, true consistency is the act of returning to your craft, again and again, with clear intention. As long as you keep showing up, you haven't failed; you are simply in the middle of your story.

If you keep creating, reflecting, and adjusting, you are winning, even when it doesn't look like it yet.

You Don't Need Permission to Take This Seriously

One of the most persistent myths in the digital world is that you need a specific milestone, like a thousand subscribers or an official brand partnership, before you can truly call yourself a "creator." In reality, you don't need any external validation to treat this as meaningful, professional work. You are allowed to care deeply about your channel from day one, and you are allowed to build it at a pace that fits your life, even if that means moving slowly and learning in public.

Whether your YouTube journey ultimately becomes a passionate side project, a creative outlet, or a full-time career, the effort you invest today is never wasted. Beyond the views and the metrics, the process of creating content teaches you a high-level set of skills that translate into almost every area of life. Every time you hit "record" or "publish," you are practicing the art of clear communication, the structure of storytelling, the management of complex systems, and the discipline of a consistent schedule.

Most importantly, you are building self-trust. By showing up for your ideas and seeing them through to completion, you are proving to yourself that you can master new challenges. These are the "hidden" benefits of being a creator, and they remain valuable regardless of where your channel goes next.

How to Use This Book Going Forward

This isn't a one-time read. Come back to it when:

- You feel stuck or overwhelmed.
- Your motivation dips.
- You're unsure what to improve next.
- You want to reset your workflow.
- You need a reminder that progress is non-linear.

Revisit the checklists. Reuse the planners. Update your reflection tracker.

Let this book be a **tool**, not a test you pass once and forget.

One Final Reminder

As you reach the end of this journey, it is important to remember that the goal was never to achieve perfection within thirty days. True mastery on YouTube doesn't come from a lack of mistakes; it comes from the persistence to keep moving forward despite them. The real objective was simply to become the kind of person who keeps going, and by reaching this final page, you have already proven that you are exactly that person.

Your channel is a living thing that will naturally evolve as you do. With every upload, your confidence will grow, your technical skills will sharpen, and your unique voice will become clearer. This transformation doesn't happen all at once; it happens slowly, deliberately, and consistently, one video at a time.

You have the tools, the knowledge, and the mindset you need to succeed. Now, the most important step is the one you take next. Close this book, step in front of the camera, and keep creating.

www.ingramcontent.com/pod-product-compliance
Ingram Content Group UK Ltd.
Pitfield, Milton Keynes, MK11 3LW, UK
UKHW021036270726
13967UKWH00013B/2806